Many Christians struggle with the modern workplace – how to deal with its challenges and temptations, while seeking to serve God faithfully and live out their calling in the world. *Proving Ground* is true to its title. You will be tested and tried but also buoyed and encouraged by the practical examples and thoughtful questions presented in this helpful book.

IAN HARPER, AO
Professor of Economics and
Dean of Melbourne Business School,
Melbourne, Australia

Is there significance in my work? The answers are in these pages! *Proving Ground* identifies our biblical and unique value in our everyday living, breathing, working life – no matter where we find ourselves between the working hours of 9-5, overnight, shift or casual work! This book will invite and challenge you to bring the truth of Christ into your work, through and in all types of situations and scenarios. *Proving Ground* shows us that our working life can be an extension of our 'Beyond Sunday' posture, full of meaning, purpose and destiny. Every Christian in the marketplace needs to read this book – it will change us, our work places and our world!

BERNADETTE BLACK, AM
Founding Director, CEO, Brave Foundation
Author, Speaker and Ambassador

In *Proving Ground*, Graham Hooper has written one of the most accessible and practical books I have ever read in the space of Christian faith at work. The topics are thoughtfully organized to reflect the difficulties and opportunities that everyday working Christians face in vocational life. Using a biblical context, Graham offers actionable advice covering everything from motives to methods. No matter your line of work, this book will work wonders for you in bridging theory and practice for the faith active working Christian.

CHUCK PROUDFIT
President, At Work on Purpose, Cincinnati, Ohio, USA

I have known Graham Hooper for several years. Over that time there have been two issues that he has been consistently passionate about when it comes to Christians and the workplace – that Biblical teaching address all types of workers (not just the so-called white collar professionals), and that all Christians recognise that the workplace may be more about what God is doing in us (than what we might believe we are doing for Him). So it is a delight to see these two issues come together in this practical, personal, and passionate book. With short, 'bite-sized' chapters, this is the perfect read for the busy worker. Be encouraged by Graham's example and Biblical insights. Be challenged by his questioning of our priorities. But whatever you do, be sure to read and reflect deeply on this book, and be open to how God might change you (as He did me!) in reading it.

ANDREW LAIRD
Life@Work National Manager, City Bible Forum

This is an excellent book, it will fill a large gap in contemporary Christian literature, to provide practical guidance referenced from lived experience of being a Christian in the everyday world of work. For many Christians the world of work is rarely the centre of Sunday worship and teaching, yet it occupies most of our time, relationships and attention. In *Proving Ground*, I particularly like the way Graham Hooper has woven real story from his own diverse work journey with well-chosen biblical references so the reader can immediately understand what Jesus or Paul was saying and revealing its relevance in the context of work, whether it's about the boss, a work colleague, organisational culture, the ethics of the corporation etc. It's a bit like reading the Bible through a work lens.

This approach will be so helpful for Christian men and women who in their various work and career assignments may struggle with the challenge and expectation that their faith ought to be relevant and life giving for the people they work with and for themselves as they endeavour to make work a place where they can naturally express their deepest sense of calling and identity.

GEORGE SAVVIDES, AM
Career CEO, Chair SBS Australia

As a business leader who seeks to live out my faith in my everyday life, I am always delighted to find a book which enriches my ability to reflect more intentionally on how God is using the situations in my worklife to disciple and shape me. Graham Hooper's book, *Proving Ground,* is a welcome addition to a growing number of books being written to encourage the Faith@Work movement.

I have noticed younger workers are often keen to find mentors who have real life experience of answering those important questions: 'How did you navigate office politics?' 'How do I use my ambition positively?' 'As a Christian how do I handle conflict with my fellow-workers?' I commend this book to every experienced business leader, it will help you shape your legacy as a Marketplace Christian. In writing this book, Graham is walking the talk, he's taking a Kingdom minded approach to why God has been using the workplace to shape his Christian experience. Graham has taken the time to reflect on his own proving ground experiences and through this process he gives us a framework to help readers reflect on what we've actually learned during our own life-shaping process in the workplace.

Sometimes as seasoned leaders with the pressure of business we have pressed on, moving from one project to the next, without drawing out the gold nuggets of learning which are real assets to be shared with others. Reading this book has reminded me that God isn't just shaping us, proving us, for our own personal benefit, but so we can disciple and mentor others. Grab your own copy and a stack of copies for all those who look to you for leadership, you'll be glad you did.

WENDY SIMPSON, OAM
Chair, Wengeo Group Pty Ltd.
Founding Chair, SBE Australia
Non-Executive Director, World Vision Australia

Graham brings together a thoughtful Christian perspective and a knowledgeable business perspective to important issues of faith and work. There are many Christians thinking through how their faith can and does interact with their daily work. In Graham, Christians will find someone who asks questions, just as a mentor would, and provides stories that will help them find their own answers. Graham Hooper spends the first part of the

book discussing a number of important issues that Christians have as they seek to discern God's calling for them through their work. A section follows this which deals with qualities that Christians can bring to any job. It was particularly apposite to see these qualities described through the lens of God's attributes and our role as image-bearers and ambassadors for Christ. The third section of the book focuses on relationships. Dealing with team members, colleagues, bosses and difficult clients is a staple of any workplace. This important section gives great advice and help to Christians struggling to navigate relationships. Fourthly, Graham outlines a number of difficult dilemmas and critical situations that Christians may find themselves in at work. He covers everything from boredom to bullying: situations that may derail a Christian's witness and wellbeing. The book reflects on biblical models and responses to these situations in ways that I believe readers will find encouraging. The final section puts it all together with uplifting thoughts about seeing the big picture. This book isn't just for individuals. If there are home groups and book groups looking for something to read about the workplace, this book will be a very fruitful choice. I would recommend *Proving Ground* for Christian groups to work through together, with useful discussion starters provided throughout.

JENNY GEORGE
CEO, Converge International

Why does our work matter? How can we live out our faith authentically at work? How can we be salt and light in our workplaces and point our colleagues to Christ? So often churches neglect the world of work, leaving Christians to figure out all this on their own. But in *Proving Ground*, Graham Hooper has written a terrifically helpful book that tackles all these questions and more. Graham's book will help you get excited about the workplace where God has called you – and will equip, challenge, and stretch you to apply your faith in Christ to that environment. In Colossians, Paul writes of the need to be 'wise in the way you act toward unbelievers ... making the most of every opportunity.' This book will help you do that and be a Monday-to-Saturday Christian, not just a Sunday Christian.

ANDY BANNISTER
Director of Solas (Centre for Public Christianity), UK

PROVING GROUND

40 REFLECTIONS ON
GROWING FAITH AT WORK

GRAHAM HOOPER

CHRISTIAN
FOCUS

Copyright © Graham Hooper 2022

Paperback ISBN 978-1-5271-0845-5
E-book ISBN 978-1-5271-0921-6

10 9 8 7 6 5 4 3 2 1

Published in 2022
by
Christian Focus Publications Ltd,
Geanies House, Fearn, Ross-shire,
IV20 1TW, Great Britain.

www.christianfocus.com

A CIP catalogue record for this book is available from the British Library.

Cover design by James Amour

Printed by Bell & Bain, Glasgow

Contents

Foreword

It was the most memorable doctor's appointment I've ever had. I'd never met him before but immediately after I'd sat down across from his desk, he said, 'Before you tell me what you've come in for, would you mind standing up for a moment?'

He came round the other side of the desk, asked me to move something this way, and something else that way, and then said: 'I think you have a hernia.' It turned out I did. And it was dealt with long, long before it caused me any pain, or discomfort, or inconvenienced anyone at work or at home at all seriously. I hadn't gone to see the doctor about any pain anywhere near where that hernia was. But there it was. I was amazed, grateful. Good doctors are alert to possibilities. And they want the best for you.

Graham has clearly written this book because he wants God's best for us at work—whatever that work is. It is a book about working well for God, being our best at work for God, doing our best at work for God, serving our colleagues well for God, serving the organisation well for God. To His glory. And its focus is on the things that might get in the way of that, and how we might, with God's help and other people's encouragement, do something about them.

Graham assumes we know that work is significant to God, that it's central to His plans for human beings, that it's one of the ways God wants people created in His image to serve others, bring order, provision, joy, beauty, and release potential to His Glory. And Graham rightly assumes that God, the master discipler, will use our work to disciple us to grow more like His son. But we live in a fallen world. Challenges abound. And Graham has had decades of experience in a range of countries in industries where some of the work is downright dangerous and is conducted in searing heat or ice-in-the-marrow cold.

He is neither naively triumphalistic about how Christians can walk the way of Jesus at work, nor gloomily pessimistic. He doesn't problematise work or demonise corporations or institutions but he doesn't duck the big issues, sidestep the hard questions, or ignore the reality that some of us have to work with difficult, ornery, tetchy, downright unpleasant people. Or that we might not be paragons of perfection ourselves. You can see this right there in the contents page. There's helpful biblical material on boredom as well as creativity, on setbacks as well as success, on being trapped in less than interesting work, with no apparent way out. This isn't just a book for high-flying graduate execs but for people engaged in all kinds of work. Of course, not all the issues Graham covers are ones that you may think you particularly need help with. I didn't. But just as I didn't think I had a hernia, I discovered more issues than I realised. Pride? Moi?

Still, Graham doesn't wag his finger at us. He encourages us. He lays out an issue, gives us a biblical framework, often a biblical example. He gives us examples from his own working life and from people he's met, and he testifies to the difference that God's Word, God's prompting, God's interventions have made. Along the way he asks questions, and at the end of each chapter too. Sometimes the questions are challenging, sometimes deceptively simple. 'What kind of leader are you?' was the one that got me thinking, got me wondering what I thought, what others thought, what God thought.

What kind of worker are you?

What kind of worker would you like to be?

What kind of worker could you become with God's help?

This book is a rich resource for all those questions. And it's warm, witty, wise, biblical, personal, and kind. A gift really. Envious? Me? Maybe a smidgen. Grateful. Definitely.

MARK GREENE
London Institute for Contemporary Christianity
UK

Preface

I have wanted to write this book for a while. It started when I realised that it was forty years ago that I came to faith in Christ and forty years since I began full-time work. My job has taken me to live for extended periods in six different countries and to work in some twenty more. A good time, I thought, to reflect on lessons learned and the difference that being a Christian has made to my life.

But I have wanted to write for a second reason. I have read many books (and listened to many talks) about the opportunity and challenge of relating Christian faith to daily work. Most of them seem to me to be directed to the professional middle-classes with reasonably well paid and fulfilling jobs. Many of them focus more on the creative and fulfilling aspects of work than on its hardships. But I wonder ... what good news is being offered to the labourers working twelve-hour shifts in 40 degree heat in the Arabian Gulf, or workers in the massive garment and electronics factories in Asia, or the unemployed in the back streets of the megacities of the world? What about those in later life, looking back and wondering what they have achieved that is worthwhile, wondering whether they have missed out on God's best for their lives?

Thank God, the Bible's teaching about work is *inclusive*. Paul wrote about work to churches which included slaves, those denied freedom and trapped in situations with limited opportunities to escape. It's hard to think of a more demeaning and less satisfying role. But the Bible is *a message of good news* with a universal application. It's also *honest and realistic* about the problems and pressures of daily work and the way these often test our faith in a just and loving God.

It's this truly biblical view of work, grounded in my own work experience, which I have tried to present in this book. I hope you will enjoy the read.

Acknowledgements

I would like to acknowledge gratefully all the friends and colleagues I have known who have shown me what it means to live out their Christian faith in their daily work—often in testing situations. I have drawn heavily on their wisdom and experiences in this book. In several cases I have changed their names to respect privacy.

A big 'thank you' to Mark Greene for writing the Foreword and for being an inspirer and supporter over many years. Thanks also to David Jackman for his encouragement and guidance; Gina Denholm, and Andrew Laird for reviewing early drafts; to Matthew Turnour for allowing me to test some of this material with his team over several lunch hour sessions; to Peter Adam for his advice on some theological issues, to Wendy Simpson for her prayers, encouragement and advice; to Ian Harper, Bernadette Black, Jenny George, Chuck Proudfit, Willy Kotiuga and George Savvides for their supporting comments; to Dr Mark Hooper for his wise insights; and to my wife Sue for patiently and lovingly supporting me through the process of getting this book written.

I thank my God every time I remember you all (Phil. 1:3).

GRAHAM HOOPER

Introduction

Proving and testing

There is no such thing as untested Christian faith.

Testing is part of Christian experience. Not in the sense that God sets us tests we have to pass to qualify to be Christian. If He did, none of us would make the grade! But our Christian faith is tested and 'proved' *in life generally* when we face sickness, bereavement and family problems, or when we experience doubt, depression or injustice. We naturally start wondering, 'Is God really there? Does He care about my life? Why do I have to wait so long for God to answer my prayers?'

As we spend most of our waking hours working, whether at home, in voluntary work, study or in a paid job, it follows that our faith will be tested in our *work*. It's there we have to deal with long hours, stress and difficult people. At work we face tests of our honesty. We may make mistakes, fail, and get our priorities wrong. Will we remember to thank God in the good times? Will we trust God when the going gets tough? Will we compromise our values when it suits us? Do we love people as Jesus commanded us, or use them as stepping stones to our own success? Will our faith prove to be true and lasting, or just religious talk?

But isn't 'testing' a negative thing? Aren't testing experiences often difficult, unpleasant or even traumatic. I never enjoyed exams at school. I don't enjoy having blood tests, X-rays or more invasive medical tests. I certainly wouldn't like to have to re-take my driving test! Isn't God's 'testing' an experience we would rather avoid if we want to enjoy life? So, if we are trying to live out Christian faith at work, why not just concentrate on opportunities to use our gifts and talents. Why not emphasise the more attractive aspects like creativity, rewards and fulfilment? Wouldn't this be a much more positive approach?

But the reality is that every Christian experiences God's 'testing' in one way or another. According to the Bible, it's part of the lifelong process of being changed by the Spirit of God to become more like Jesus, (1 Thess. 4:3; 2 Cor. 3:18). God's purpose is to produce 'gold' in terms of Christ-like character from the unpromising raw material of our lives.

So God's testing is not a 'negative'. It is an essential part of God's work in our lives. It's more like the very necessary road testing of a new vehicle on a 'proving ground'. How does it perform under actual driving conditions and in all weathers? Will it hold together? Will it last, or will it fall apart? Our work, like every part of our life, is a 'proving ground' for our faith, a place where we learn more about God, and more about ourselves.

But this 'proving' works both ways. As we learn to trust God, we prove for ourselves that God is faithful and that His Word is true, even when the cards all seem stacked against us. In the words of Psalm 34 we 'taste and see that that the LORD is good'. More than that, with God's help, we start to show by the way we work, how we treat people and how we deal with difficulties, that God is real and that He is at work in His world for good.

This applies to *every* Christian. The gospel is good news for all of us, and it speaks to every part of our life.

Testing in the Bible (refer also to Appendix: 'the biblical language of "testing" and "proving"')

In the Bible we find that testing has always been part of the experience of God's people. In our English Bibles, depending on the translation, the most commonly used verbs are:

'prove', 'try', 'examine', 'probe', 'test', 'tempt', 'refine'.[1]

---

1. **In the Old Testament**, the Hebrew words (and their various forms and derivatives) most commonly used are *bachan*, *nasah* and *tsaraph*. These three words appear together in Psalm 26. Motyer comments on this verse: 'The 3 verbs for testing here are broadly synonymous. If distinction is possible, then "test" (*bachan*) is to test for purity, reality, reliability; "try" (*nasah*), is to test circumstantially for fidelity and to "assay" (*tsaraph*) is to test for impurity, specifically of precious metal, to refine' ('Psalms by the Day', Alec Motyer, (Christian Focus, 2016)).

In the New Testament the two key words are *dokimon* and *peirasmos* and their various forms; e.g. 'Dokimazo'; ... prove to be the real thing, something of real value. *Peirasmos* seems to refer mainly to trials and difficulties experienced by

Testing in the Bible seems to come in three ways:

- **God's probing and revealing;**
- **testing and refining; and**
- **temptation**

1. Probing and revealing

The Israelites' commitment to their God was tested like this as they wandered through the desert before they entered the Promised Land:

> *'Remember how the LORD your God led you all the way in the wilderness these forty years, to humble and test you, in order to know what was in your heart, whether or not you would keep his commands'* (Deut. 8:2).

God's probing of our hearts and revealing of our true selves, is a strong theme in the psalms, with their repeated reminders that God knows us because He made us. He knows how we are wired, and therefore we need to be honest with Him and honest with ourselves (see for example Pss. 103 and 139).

It's also a recurring theme in the prophetic books of the Old Testament (particularly Jeremiah), where the prophet's words cut through the complacency, misplaced confidence and hypocrisy of the people; for example *'You Lord Almighty who judge righteously and test the heart and mind ...'* (Jer. 11:20)[2] and *'Yet you know me Lord, you see me and test my thoughts about you'* (12:3). When King David was encouraging his son Solomon to stay faithful to the Lord he reminded him that *'the Lord searches every heart and understands every desire and every thought'* (1 Chron. 28:9). Later, when King Hezekiah, distracted by his riches, power and success, failed to trust God in a crunch moment, we are told: *'God left him to test him and to know everything that was in his heart'* (2 Chron. 32:31).

In the New Testament we find a similar focus on God probing our hearts to show us the real state of our lives and the depth of our

---

God's people though it is also used to mean 'temptation' (James 1:12,14). The two words occur together in James 1:2-4.

2. See also Jeremiah 12:3; 17:10; 20:12.

understanding and faith. Jesus tested Philip's faith in Him in this way. Could Jesus miraculously provide bread for a huge crowd of people in the wilderness, just as God had done for the people in Moses' time? *Jesus said to Philip 'Where shall we buy bread for these people to eat? He asked this only to test him, for he already had in mind what he was going to do'* (John 6:5, 6).

This form of 'testing' by God is a reminder that He sees into the hearts of everyone, good and bad, believers and non-believers. He wants to show us the true state of our lives, so that we know ourselves, and more importantly, learn more about our righteous, holy, loving, faithful God in the process.

This probing and testing by God into our lives therefore finds a positive response in the hearts of His people in the form of a deep longing to live openly and transparently. So Paul urges believers to 'test' (examine) themselves in preparing to share in the Lord's Supper (1 Cor. 11:28), and to *'examine yourselves to see whether you are in the faith ...'* (2 Cor. 13:5).

As the psalmist prayed: *'Search me, God and know my heart; test me and know my anxious thoughts. See if there is any offensive way in me and lead me in the way everlasting'* (Ps. 139:23, 24).

2. Testing and refining

This sort of testing is more than God's gentle probing. It's ratcheted up a notch. This is about God building our faith in Him, and changing us for good, through stressful and adverse circumstances.

The Israelites were tested like this as they wandered through the desert before they entered the Promised Land. For forty years, life was not easy. The future was uncertain. They doubted God knew what He was doing, if He was there at all. They rebelled, they turned to idolatry and rejected God's appointed leaders. The people grumbled and even longed to go back to slavery in Egypt. They wouldn't trust God to provide for them, or to enable them to defeat their enemies. As they were finally about to enter the Promised Land, Moses gets the people to look back at this prolonged testing experience. He reminds them that though they had repeatedly failed the tests (Deut. 8), God's purpose was all for their good:

'He gave you manna to eat in the wilderness ... to humble and test you so that in the end it might go well with you' (Deut. 8:16).

The wisdom literature of The Old Testament includes the lengthy account of Job's sufferings, his tested faith and his conviction that God would bring him through, *'But he knows the way that I take; when he has tested me, I will come forth as gold'* (Job 23:10).

As Gregory Smith comments, 'the Bible is not shy in presenting its heroes as they experience the refinement of faith through suffering and trial. In fact, the Bible invites us to see ourselves in their stories.'[3]

The New Testament continues the Old Testament theme of God's people being tested through hard experiences.

Jesus told the story of two houses, one built on rock and the other on sand. The strength of each foundation is tested when storms come. The point of the story? When our faith is tested by adverse circumstances, will we still stand strong or collapse in a heap? Will we listen to, and put into practice, Jesus' words and so build on 'the rock', or will we ignore them, and so build on 'the sand' (Matt. 7:24-27)?

Paul applies the Old Testament account of the Israelites' journey through the desert to Christian experience. He warns believers of the dangers of missing out on God's salvation just as an entire generation of Israelites (Caleb and Joshua excepted) missed out on entering the Promised Land. Specifically he warned of *'setting our hearts on evil things'* (1 Cor. 10:6). Then, he promises: *'God is faithful he will not let you be tempted* (NIV footnote: tested) *beyond what you can bear. But when you are tempted he will also provide a way out so that you can endure it'* (1 Cor. 10:13). He also reassures Christian believers that *'In all things God works for the good of those who love him ...'* (Rom. 8:28).

The New Testament generally teaches us that Christians can expect to be tested through difficult experiences, but in the wisdom of God, such testing is revealing, productive and fruitful. So, James encouraged his readers:

'Consider it pure joy, my brothers and sisters, whenever you face trials of many kinds, because you know that the testing of your

---

3. Gregory S. Smith, *The testing of God's Sons* (B&H Publishing Group, 2014), p. xvii.

faith produces perseverance. Let perseverance finish its work so that you may be mature and complete, not lacking anything' (James 1:2-4).

Similarly, the Apostle Peter taught the early Christians that the tests they faced, particularly persecution, were part of God's 'proving' work in their lives, like a refiner producing gold:

> *'These (trials) have come so that the proven genuineness of your faith—of greater worth than gold, which perishes even though refined by fire—may result in praise, glory and honour when Jesus Christ is revealed'* (1 Pet. 1:7).

J. I. Packer, helpfully summarised the biblical view of testing like this:

> *'God tests his people by putting them in situations which reveal the quality of their faith and devotion so that all can see what is in their hearts* (Gen. 22:1; Exod. 16:4, 20:20; Deut. 7:2, 16; 13:3; Judg. 2:22; 2 Chron. 32:31). *By thus making trial of them he purifies them, as metal is purified in the refiner's crucible* (Ps. 66:10; Isa. 48:10; Zech. 13:9; 1 Pet. 1:6f.; cf. Ps. 119:67, 71); *he strengthens their patience and matures their Christian character* (James 1:2ff, 12; cf 1 Pet. 5:10); *and he leads them into an enlarged assurance of his love for them* (Gen. 22:15ff; Rom. 5:3ff). *Through faithfulness in the time of trial people become "dokimoi, approved" in God's sight'.*[4]

In the early years of our married life, my wife and I became friends with a woman who held down a senior full-time job with a government education department. She was also primary carer for a sick, elderly friend, who in old age had become extremely difficult and demanding. In a busy, stressful life, our friend somehow found time to help out at a children's home, to chair the local Bible Society and play a lead role in her local church. On her table she kept a card printed with this verse:

> *Pressed by the sorrows that each day brings*
> *Pressed into faith for impossible things*
> *Pressed into looking each day to the Lord*
> *Pressed into living a Christ-life outpoured*

---

4. 'Temptation', J. I. Packer *New Bible Dictionary*, Third Edition (IVP, 1996).

This lady was continually having her faith tested, through the pressures of daily life, but she saw God's testing as a positive in her life. The result was a Christ-like life which blessed us and all who knew her.

3. Temptation

This form of testing is one we all experience in one form or another, every day. The words 'temptation' and 'testing' are sometimes used interchangeably in our English Bibles. But this is not God's testing. Temptation comes from Satan, described by Jesus as 'the evil one'.

The New Testament letter of James speaks a lot about testing and makes this distinction very clear:

> 'When tempted, no one should say "God is tempting me". For God cannot be tempted by evil. Nor does he tempt anyone, but each person is tempted when they are dragged away by their own evil desire and enticed' (James 1:13-14).

Jesus was tested like this over a period of forty days in the Judean wilderness before beginning His three years of ministry which changed history (Matt. 4). He was tempted by Satan to chase after power, material wealth and fame, rather than live the life and die the death to which God His Father had called Him.

So, we are tempted, and often fail. Temptations come in different forms and in different intensities at different stages of our lives. They find a 'hook' into our lives when we give in to them. We never outgrow our susceptibility to give in to temptation in this life, to follow 'the devices and desires of our own hearts'.[5] That's why Jesus taught us to pray every day: 'Lead us not into temptation but deliver us from the evil one' (Matt. 6:13).

We will certainly be tempted in one way or another at work. Thank God … He is the supreme power and can even use those temptations (and our failures) for good. And, let's remember that our God offers forgiveness, restoration and a new start when we fail.

Whether it's God's probing and revealing, refining, or temptation to sin, all of us experience these three forms of testing. In this book I

---

5. 'Book of Common Prayer,' 1662.

want to reflect on how we experience this testing *in our work* and how we deal with it.

For me, and I suspect for all Christians, this is a continuing learning experience.

Learning lessons

My first experience of work (outside the home) was carting manure, tipping it into piles and spreading it by pitchfork to enrich the soil. I was working in a large market garden (aka garden centre). I was fourteen years old and took the job to save money to buy a bike. I was entirely motivated by a need for money. Given a choice I would rather have spent my holidays playing soccer with my mates in the park.

I learned three life lessons in this short experience. I learned about the value of money, how hard it is to earn and how easy to spend! My pay rate was low. In modern terms it was less than the hourly equivalent of the price of a 'Big Mac'. I had to work for four weeks to buy the modest second-hand bike I wanted. I also learned a lot about manual work, discovering muscles I didn't know I had and thinking 'there must be more to life than this'. At the same time I found myself enjoying physical labour in the open air and getting satisfaction from finishing my task. Most importantly, I learned to respect working people—as I sat down every morning for a late breakfast, talking with those who worked there full time, I realised that though I would be back at school after the holidays, this was their life. They had to work.

Our family did not have a lot of money, so like many students, I spent a lot of weekends and holidays stacking supermarket shelves, loading trucks and labouring on building sites. I learned a lot from those different experiences of hard, manual and sometimes boring work. This, after all, is the experience of the great majority of people in this world.

Later, in my twenties, I was living in a tent, working in a remote location in the Selous Game Reserve in southern Tanzania. I had a lot of time to think and to read in the African bush. One evening, I started to read the New Testament—it was an unopened hardback version, received as a prize at school. I had only packed it in my gear because I thought it would be useful for pressing flat my family photos! Perversely, I started to read at the end, in the book of Revelation. I still

remember the mind-blowing impact of the words: *"'I am the Alpha and the Omega," says the Lord God, "who is, and who was, and who is to come, the Almighty"'* (Rev. 1:8). God had begun it all. God would end it all. God was holding it all together. He was the ultimate frame of reference for life. Around the same time, I received a long letter from a friend who had become a Christian. He urged me to read the Bible! God was at work. It was a life-changing period and the beginning of a whole new process of learning.

I thought at the time that this was just the end of a search for meaning in life. I gradually discovered it was a new beginning. I learned that when we start to trust and follow Christ, our attitude to life changes. We discover that we *'were bought at a price'* (1 Cor. 6:20). We belong to the Christ who died for us. As we start this new life, we find that 'belonging' to Christ, far from constraining our lives, brings an experience of freedom and fulfilment. We become the people God has called us to be, the people that, in our best moments at least, we want to be.

Still, it took me a while to discover that God was interested in my work, home life and leisure as well as in my 'spiritual' life. It took me even longer to realise, through some 'hard knocks', that we grow in our faith through facing difficult issues and taking on new challenges, because it is then that we learn to rely on God, rather than just on our own resources.

As I started to read the Bible, I began to discover a lot more about how my new-found Christian faith related to my daily work. I started to learn that:

- Work provides a great opportunity to 'live out' our faith, recognising that God is at work in us and in His world.

- Work provides the biggest and best opportunity to do this, given that this is how we spend most of our waking hours.

- At work our faith is tested, not in the sense of being tested to give up believing, nor in the sense of God giving us hurdles to jump over, but rather in *proving* in our own experience, and in the midst of difficult situations, that God is real, that what we read in the Bible is true, and that our daily work is

as much an opportunity to honour God as what we say and do in church on Sunday.[6]

As a civil engineer in the infrastructure business, I have had the privilege of living for extended periods in different countries. I have had some great times, experienced satisfaction and fulfilment in my work and made many good friends. My work has provided opportunities for creativity, innovation, and given me the satisfaction that comes from a job well-done. Through work I have been able to provide for my family. But I have also been stressed, frustrated and exhausted. I have seen the destructive effects of exploitation and corruption, experienced setbacks and failure, learned some hard lessons about patience and persistence and, at times, questioned the worth of what I was doing.

At work, my faith continues to be tested.

A Proving Ground for Faith

If work is a 'proving ground' for our Christian faith, how does the 'road testing' of our professed beliefs stand up to the long miles, the heavy traffic and wear and tear of everyday life, particularly life at work?

Reflecting on my own experiences, and those of many friends and workmates, I have come to see God's testing in these five areas:

> **Understanding our Motives:** I may claim to be 'working for the Lord' but what does that mean in practice?
>
> **Living our Values:** Do I actually live out the values I profess to hold to as a Christian?
>
> **Transforming Relationships:** What difference has my faith made to the way I treat people? Do I show something of the love of Christ or turn people off?
>
> **Testing Situations:** How do I act and react when the going gets tough?
>
> **Keeping our focus:** As I reflect on my experience of work, have I kept sight of the big picture—what God is doing in the world?

---

6. Kara Martin helpfully coined the word 'Workship' to make the point that work is part of our worship of God.

The forty short chapters that make up this book are grouped under the headings of these proving grounds for Christian faith. Forty seems a neat number, given its strong association in the Bible with testing and proving faith and commitment. The Israelites were in the wilderness for forty years. Jesus was tested for forty days (Matt. 4:1-2).

In each of these areas I want to explore how we experience testing, whether in the form of God's probing and revealing, in difficult circumstances or through temptation, and how, at the same time, we prove the reality and goodness of God in our own experience—and grow in the process.

In each chapter I have tried to share something of the challenge, and the encouragement, that I have found in the Scriptures in seeking to live out my faith. You might like to use some of these chapters for group or personal study,[7] or you may prefer just to read right through, or dip in and out of the topics that interest you most.

Maybe you are finding that being a Christian at work is a much more testing experience than you had expected.

Maybe you have come to Christian faith after beginning your working life (as I did) and are trying to work out how your new faith will affect your work.

Maybe you are still keeping your working life locked up in a different compartment to your Christian faith.

Maybe you have lost sight of the big picture of how God is at work in our work!

The subtitle of this book '40 Reflections on Growing Faith at Work' tells you what you will find in it: reflections on what I have learned from the Bible, and in daily life, about the way God uses testing experiences in our work to grow our faith and transform our character. I doubt you will agree with all my comments, but I hope this book helps you reflect honestly on the Scriptures and on your own experience. I hope that it encourages you, particularly in the hard times, to remember that testing is common to every Christian and

---

7. Several of the studies in Part A 'Understanding our Motives' have been used in lunchtime studies by groups of Christians in their secular workplaces.

is part of God's good plan for our lives in making us the people He wants us to be … and to remember that He '*is able to keep you from stumbling and to present you before his glorious presence without fault and with great joy*' (Jude 24).

Above all, I hope you prove in your life the reality, presence, power and faithfulness of God.

PART A

UNDERSTANDING OUR MOTIVES

> *'Nearly all the wisdom we possess, that is to say true and sound wisdom, consists of two parts: the knowledge of God and of ourselves … it is certain that man never achieves a clear knowledge of himself unless he has first looked upon God's face, and then descends from contemplating him to scrutinizing himself.'*[1] JOHN CALVIN

Calvin wrote those wise words nearly 500 years ago. He understood from the Bible that part of God's work in our lives is to probe deeply into our hearts and minds, to test our motives and our values, to make us aware of our strengths and weaknesses; in other words to help us know ourselves better as we get to know God better through His Word.

To reflect on our motives for work, or for any part of life, is not therefore a matter of indulging in fruitless navel-gazing. If we want to live with integrity, we need to understand ourselves, to bring our motives out into the light of the Word of God, to ask God to renew our minds and transform our approach to work. Ask yourself:

- Why am I doing the work I am doing?
- Why do I work longer and harder than I need to?
- What gets me out of bed in the mornings?

We may claim to be 'working for the Lord' but what other motives are driving us and how do they align with our desire to honour God in our work?

What motivates us to work? What motivates us to work better, harder, longer? How do these motives fit with Christian faith? Scratch the surface of a professing Christian and you are likely to find a whole

---

1. John Calvin, *Institutes of the Christian Religion*; 1:1:2, pp. 35-37.

mix of factors, some godly and some driven by human self-centredness. Ask five people, doing exactly the same job, what motivates them to work well and you may well get five different answers. Try it!

Our motives, whatever they are, are likely to change over time. In our twenties we may be motivated by adventure, by the urge to put a foot on the corporate or academic ladder, or by being part of a group of people who want to make a difference to our world. Or, maybe, we just want to make enough money to be able to move into our own place. Later in life, our focus might shift to earning enough to raise a family and saving for the future. In retirement, many sign up for voluntary work with the intention of using their skills and 'giving something back'.

So, as we think through some of these issues in the following chapters, we might pray with the psalmist: '*Search me God and know my heart ...*' (Ps. 139:23).

1. Necessity

'I owe, I owe, it's off to work I go'[2]

Why work? Ask that question of the young couple with a huge mortgage, a car loan, maxed out credit cards or, even worse, with predatory loan sharks beating at their door. Ask the builder's labourer working long hours in the freezing cold or extreme heat, or the Filipina housemaid working on the Arabian Peninsula, separated from her children. Ask the shift worker from the 'Projects' on the south side of Chicago, the African male working night shifts in the mines, or the subsistence farmer in the Cambodian rice fields. The question itself is a 'no-brainer'. 'I work because I have to … I need the money … otherwise my family would starve.' That would be the automatic response.

If you have an interesting, and physically or mentally engaging job that gives you satisfaction, thank God and thank the people who have sacrificed to give you an education which has opened up opportunities for you. Most people don't have that privilege. There are millions locked into a treadmill of working at low paid jobs because they have to. Those whose main focus at work is to plot a way of escape at the end of their shift or at the end of their week.

My first job after graduation was for the Game Department in Tanzania. I supervised work teams, building roads and airstrips to open up the Selous game reserve for hunting safaris. For me, it was a big adventure. For most of the workers it was a matter of necessity. When I went to inspect the work at each site, I would greet the builders with the traditional Swahili greeting, 'Jambo, habari za kazi?' … 'Hi there,

---

2. Popular car sticker slogan which parodies the working song of the seven dwarfs in Disney's *Snow White*.

how is work going?' The polite reply was to say that 'work was good'. But often I got a different response ... 'Kazi ipo', literally 'Work ... it's there'. That response sums up the daily experience of work for most people on this planet ... 'work? It's there'. 'Work? Meh! I have to do it. Why bother even asking me about it?'

How did these people find meaning in their work? It was not so much the work itself, rather the prospect of release at the end of each month: the 'Thank God it's Friday' syndrome translated into the African bush. On pay-day, everyone would pile into the back of a five-tonne truck for the long bumpy ride into town. They left camp after a month of hard work, the young ones cashed-up, and looking for excitement, the older guys relieved that their family would eat that month.

Necessity is the most basic motivator to work. What can prevent that need becoming drudgery? What can transform the *necessity* of work into something meaningful and rewarding? What difference can being a Christian make to our attitude and our experience?

The bad news

Work is tough. The Genesis story in the Bible makes clear that work was meant to be creative and enjoyable. Life in the Garden of Eden was good. That all changed after Adam and Eve's disobedience when God decreed that; *'Cursed is the ground because of you: through painful toil you will eat food from it all the days of your life ... By the sweat of your brow you will eat your food ...'* (Gen. 3:17, 19).

And so it has been ever since. We are living in a good world gone bad. It's not usually much fun putting in a long shift on the production line, ironing clothes, dealing with difficult customers, demanding bosses, and impossible deadlines. Even in the developed economies of the world, commuting on crowded buses and trains, performing mind-numbing jobs in factories or bureaucracies, or labouring in the cold or heat, and then returning home each night exhausted, isn't particularly enjoyable. In the best of jobs, there are stresses, frustrations and disappointments, blows to our pride and challenges to our wisdom and patience, not to mention all the difficult people we have to deal with!

The good news

What good news does the Bible bring us to change our experience of work from a boring, necessary evil, something we *have* to do, into an activity that has purpose and meaning?

- Work, like life itself, is a gift from God, *'A person can do nothing better than to eat and drink and find satisfaction in their own toil. This too, I see is from the hand of God'* (Eccles. 2:24 and see also 3:9-13). God intends us to work. It is His appointed means of using and managing the resources He has built into His creation for the survival and enjoyment of human life.

- Our work can be transformed through a fundamental change of attitude: *'Serve wholeheartedly, as if you were serving the Lord, not people, because you know that the Lord will reward each one for whatever good they do, whether they are slave or free'* (Eph. 6:7-8). God is our ultimate authority and calls us to do our work for Him. Let's not pretend that this attitude suddenly turns cleaning the toilets, or collecting the rubbish into a fun activity. But it does mean I can find some satisfaction in whatever task I am doing. Martin Luther (a monk himself), applied this principle in his generation like this: 'It looks like a small thing when a maid cooks and cleans and does other housework. But because God's command is there, even such a small work must be praised as a service of God, far surpassing the holiness and asceticism of monks and nuns.'[3]

- We are to work in His name: *'Whatever you do, whether in word or deed, do it all in the name of the Lord Jesus, giving thanks to God the Father through him' (Col. 3:17).* This means we are to do our work in a way which is consistent with the character of Jesus. Each of us has to work out what that means in our particular work situation.

---

3. Martin Luther as quoted by W. R. Forrester in *Christian Vocation*, (New York, Charles Scribner's Sons, 1953), p. 148.

- We are to be different in our approach to work, seeing it and doing it as an act of worship rather than just a necessity. *'I urge you … in view of God's mercy to offer your bodies as a living sacrifice, holy and pleasing to God—this is your true and proper worship'* (Rom. 12:1).

- We are to work to support those who through age, infirmity, disability or lack of opportunity cannot work for themselves (Eph. 4:28).

- Our work is important because it is part of God's plan for us in this fallen world. *'Continue to work out your salvation with fear and trembling, for it is God who works in you to will and to act in order to fulfill his good purpose'* (Phil. 2:12-13). In other words, there is a bigger picture than just *our* attitude and motives. We are to 'work out', i.e., to live out, the life God intends us to live, knowing that God Himself is working *in us* to change our attitudes, our character and indeed our whole life. He may choose to work *through us* in achieving His great purpose. He may also be working in the lives of those we work with.

These are all great principles, but how do they work out in practice? That's the question we aim to address in the rest of this book.

Questions

1. What difference does being a Christian make to your approach to work, particularly when you are not enjoying it much?

2. What does it mean in practical terms for you to do your work 'for the Lord' (Eph. 6:17) and 'in His name' (Col. 3:17)?

3. In what ways have you experienced God at work in your work?

2. Getting Ahead

'Gain all you can ... save all you can ... give all you can' [4]
JOHN WESLEY

Wanting more

Necessity is the most obvious motivator to get us out of bed in the mornings. But what if we already earn enough for our basic needs? What motivates us to work longer and harder? Why do so many volunteer for overtime? Isn't it because we naturally want to enjoy *more* than the bare necessities of life: to live in a better apartment in a safer district, buy a car, upgrade our smartphone or take a holiday?

This particular engine is constantly driven and refuelled by advertising through the media and through peer pressure. How do you feel when your workmate is off again on holiday and you are stuck at home? Or when your neighbour announces she is moving into a new apartment and you can't even afford the place you currently have, or you are still living with your parents?

So what are our real motives for wanting to 'get ahead'? Is that desire driven simply by wanting to acquire more material possessions, or can we honestly say that we have a higher motive?

The Bible probes our motives. Jesus warned about wanting to build a comfortable life for ourselves at the expense of all else. He told the story of a rich farmer who was focused on growing his business and planning his retirement to the exclusion of any thoughts about God, or his own mortality. The farmer planned to tear down his barns to build bigger ones, to accommodate the huge store of grain that he had accumulated.

---

4. Sermon 50: Use of Money in *'The Works of John Wesley'*, ed. Thomas Jackson, 1872. n

'And I'll say to myself: "You have plenty of grain laid up for many years. Take life easy; eat, drink and be merry." But God said to him, "You fool! This very night your life will be demanded from you"' (Luke 12:19-20).

Paul warned about the love of money as an end in itself: 'But godliness with contentment is great gain. For we brought nothing into this world, and we can take nothing out of it. But if we have food and clothing, we will be content with that. Those who want to get rich fall into temptation and a trap and into many foolish and harmful desires that plunge people into ruin and destruction' (1 Tim. 6:6-9).[5]

Opportunity

But the Bible has more to say on this subject than just warning us about greed and the temptations of wealth. Work may open up great opportunities to put our God-given talents and resources to the best possible use; 'Be very careful then how you live—not as unwise but as wise, making the most of every opportunity, because the days are evil' (Eph. 5:15, 16). One commentator puts it like this: 'Like someone setting out to shop with a limited amount of money, believers have only a limited amount of time and they must spend it wisely. They are not to contribute to the evil of the days, but making the best use of time, they will redeem sections of it'.[6]

Work is not a 'time-out' from life. The clock doesn't stop while we are working. If you have just lived through the week hoping time goes quickly, then that's one week of life gone. Paul wrote about 'making the most of every opportunity' in the context of relationships and work (Ephesians chapters 5 and 6). Life is short, and we are to live wisely, and work wisely, taking opportunity to fulfil Jesus' command to love God and love our neighbour, in and through our daily work, not just outside of work.

Parents are naturally motivated to work to provide opportunities for their children, to give them the best possible start in life.

---

5. Read also Hebrews 13:5 and Proverbs 30:4.

6. Ernest Best, *Ephesians: a shorter commentary*, (T & T Clark: Edinburgh, 1993), p. 265.

My late mother worked in a sandwich bar to help support my education and I am very thankful for her. Many parents work hard and long, not so much for themselves, but so that their children can 'get ahead', escape the poverty trap and realise their full potential. We may have grown up in countries where governments provide free education right through secondary school, but many do not have that privilege. When I worked in the Middle East, I met many people from India, Pakistan, Philippines and several African countries sacrificing time with their spouses and children back home, working to earn enough to pay to keep their children at school. Office workers often keep photos of their children on their screensaver or at their workstation, a daily reminder of what is truly important to them and why they are working at all. Wanting to provide opportunities for children (or grandchildren), perhaps opportunities which the parent has been denied, keeps many at work.

In later life we may have to work to support our parents, especially in times of sickness or other hardship.[7] The Bible underlines our responsibility in this regard: *'Anyone who does not provide for their relatives, and especially for their own household, has denied the faith and is worse than an unbeliever'* (1 Tim. 5:8).

Or, we may find ourselves 'sandwiched' between having to care both for our parents and our children whilst trying to run a home and do a paid job at the same time. Help!

Giving

A test of our motives in our desire to 'get ahead' is what we do with the extra money which may come our way. Does our giving increase with our income, or does our spending go up and our giving plateau or decline? Our generosity of spirit, and our enjoyment of the blessing of God on our life, are clearly linked by this unchanging principle:

> *'Remember this: Whoever sows sparingly will also reap sparingly and whoever sows generously will also reap generously .... for God loves a cheerful giver. And God is able to bless you abundantly, so that in all things at all times, having all that you need, you will abound in every good work'* (2 Cor. 9:6-8).

---

7. See for example Jesus' teaching about supporting parents in Mark 7:9-13.

It's all about motive. Our motives reveal our heart attitude, what we really value. As the late John Stott once put it:

> 'Christians should be eager to develop their gifts, widen their opportunities, extend their influence and be given promotion in their work—not now to boost their own ego or build their own empire, but rather through everything they do to bring glory to God.'[8]

Questions

1. What motivates you to work longer or harder than is necessary to meet your basic needs? How does that fit in with your Christian faith?

2. John Wesley, the eighteenth-century evangelist, encouraged people to 'Gain all you can, save all you can, give all you can.' What do you think of this advice?

3. How do we balance the Bible's warnings about loving money and possessions with our God-given desire to use all our gifts and talents in fulfilling work?

---

8. Quoted in Alister Chapman, *Godly Ambition* (Oxford University Press, 2012), p. 156.

3. Ambition

'Ambitions for God, if they are to be worthy, can never be modest. There is something inherently inappropriate about cherishing small ambitions for God. How can we ever be content that we should acquire just a little more honour in the world?' [9]

Ambition is the desire to do something or to be someone; to reach the highest level or the most fulfilling goal achievable, with whatever abilities, resources and opportunities we have. It is the desire to 'get ahead' (see Chap. 2), but usually with a harder edge.

To be ambitious is to want to succeed. Typically it involves tenacity, perseverance, and commitment. We usually admire those who succeed to levels beyond their natural ability. We respect people who have grown up in poor or difficult circumstances who have gone on to reach the highest levels in their chosen field.

Ambition implies purpose. In that sense at least, it is totally consistent with the Christian view of life, that God has put us on this earth for a purpose: to know Him, to serve Him and to make the best of the gifts and opportunities He gives us. But this begs the question—the best for whom? For my family, my community, my country, my organisation, my church … or is it only the best for ME?

The desire to use our creative skills, and to serve people, is readily recognisable as being compatible with Christian values. But what about ambition to climb the ladder, to achieve a certain status in our chosen field? What about our natural love of praise, recognition and reward? Are these different motivating factors compatible with Christian faith? To what extent do those motives drive our behaviour? How do they align with, or conflict with the teaching of the Bible?

---

9. Chapman, p. 156.

I once listened to the CEO of a multinational corporation urge aspiring leaders to 'believe in something bigger than yourself'. This wasn't a Christian lecture, but I came away thinking that it was a pretty good guideline for a Christian's ambition at work: to focus on the bigger picture and be ambitious for something bigger than ourselves. For the Christian, that bigger 'something' is the glory of God.

Ambition can be either a creative or a destructive force. If you describe a person as 'ambitious' you could just mean that she wants to fulfil her potential and grow into bigger opportunities to exercise her skills. Equally you may be implying that she is driven, grasping and desperate to climb to the top over the backs of others. There is 'good ambition' and 'bad ambition'.

Bad ambition

According to the Bible, bad ambition is characterised by:

- seeking glory for ourselves (Matt. 20:26-27),
- love of money (1 Tim. 6:10),
- conformity to the world's standards (Rom. 12:2) and
- seeking the place of honour (Luke 14:10).

The Bible also gives us examples of bad ambition. For example, Mark's gospel tells how James and John, two of Jesus' disciples, were jockeying for position. They thought Jesus was going to bring in the Kingdom of God with all the visible trappings of worldly power. They wanted to stake their claim with their boss early, while these matters (they thought) were still up for grabs. We might describe them as 'players', 'movers and shakers'. They were ambitious for themselves.

"Teacher," they said, "we want you to do for us whatever we ask". *"What do you want me to do for you?" he asked. "Let one of us sit at your right and the other at your left in your glory"'* (Mark 10:35-37).

Jesus told them that they didn't know what they were asking. Were they really ready to pay the price of their lives, as He would have to?

Parents can be over-ambitious for their children. These two young men were clearly urged on by an equally ambitious mother. In Matthew's gospel, it's their mother who comes to Jesus with a similar request:

'Grant that one of these two sons of mine may sit at your right and the other at your left in your Kingdom' (Matt. 20:21). Not surprisingly, this level of naked ambition did not go down well with the other ten disciples (nor probably with their mothers!!) and Jesus used this opportunity to teach them yet another lesson about humility and service. Jesus clearly found their ambition for personal power and prestige to be out of order, and symptomatic of people having lost their sense of God's purpose for their lives. They are examples of 'bad ambition'.

A young businesswoman (with great honesty) expressed her struggle to reconcile her career ambitions with her Christian faith like this: *'Sometimes I feel driven by my ambition rather than me being the driver.'* She recognised that her ambition was being driven by feelings of insecurity and anxiety, rather than by wanting to please God.

Good ambition

But there is also *good ambition*, a different sort of ambition encouraged in the Bible.[10] It means 'wholehearted and energetic pursuit of the object'.[11]

Ambition in this sense is a very positive attribute. Without this sort of ambition, the world would be a sad place, full of people passively waiting for someone else to *do something!* A friend explained his motivation as being 'hard wired to want to solve problems'. This sort of good ambition is characterised by:

- passion, motivation and creative energy to complete a given task,
- confidence in the value of the task and the worth of the objective, and
- humility, in understanding our position in the big scheme of things.

For example, the Apostle Paul had the 'ambition' (lit. 'he was eagerly striving'): *'to preach the gospel where Christ was not known'* (Rom. 15:20). Specifically, Paul's ambition was to be a good steward of the gospel.

---

10. The word in the Greek original (*philotimeo*) only occurs three times in the New Testament.

11. Leon Morris, *The Epistle of Paul to the Thessalonians* (IVP, 1956), p. 81.

Paul used the same word in a different context in writing to the Christians at Thessalonica who clearly 'had issues' with work.

'Make it your ambition (lit. "eagerly strive") to lead a quiet life, to mind your own business and to work with your hands, just as we told you, so that your daily life may win the respect of outsiders and so that you will not be dependent on anybody' (1 Thess. 4:11-12).

Does that seem a strange use of the word 'ambition'? There is no suggestion of profit targets, stretch goals or awards. To 'eagerly strive' to lead a quiet life seems almost paradoxical. In context, it is about seeing daily work as part of their witness to the gospel and so working in a way which merits the respect of non-believers. Not a bad framework for our ambitions.

The third occurrence of the word is in the context of our accountability to Jesus. We can't please everyone but, *'We make it our goal (lit. "we eagerly strive") to please him'* (2 Cor. 5:9). To live to please Christ—that sounds to me like the best ambition of all.

Ambition and faith

Some Christians shy away from pursuing political or business leadership positions because they are concerned how it will affect their Christian witness. At a business group I attended while living in Dubai, we were sharing our experiences of work. One member voiced the opinion that 'for the Christian it was difficult to rise above middle management'. Why? Because, he thought that to do so they would need to act so ruthlessly in the pursuit of their ambition that they inevitably compromise their Christian values in the process. This caused vigorous debate within the group. A leading Christian businesswoman confided that her mother often expressed the same fears for her!

Of course, even good ambitions are easily spoiled by the way we pursue them. But surely this is not sufficient reason to limit ambition. Many Christian men and women hold high office in business, government and academia with great integrity. Think of Nehemiah, Joseph and Daniel in the Bible, all held very high positions of responsibility in their respective roles. Let's thank God for the 'good ambition' that God gave them.

A different type of ambition

Dave was the best man at my wedding. He was a highly successful Oxford University graduate who joined the marketing department of a major food company. After a year or so as a trainee executive, he realised that this was not the job for him. He couldn't get passionate about the corporate ambition. He told me: 'As I sat in yet another meeting with sales figures showing that our competitors were selling more chocolate than us, I realised I had to get out. There were other things I cared a lot more about.' He later became a highly respected and much-loved high school teacher in a low socio-economic inner-city area. He sadly died of colon cancer at the age of thirty-nine, but he succeeded in his calling because he really cared about the children and young people he taught. He was paid a much lower salary, but he fulfilled a new ambition, a different type of ambition, in the process.

Jane had a very different experience. She was a successful business-woman who became a Christian. Surely, she thought, God must want her to leave her job and serve in full-time Christian work. After a year's theological study, she gradually came to realise that God was calling her back into the rough and tumble of business life and to live out her faith in this challenging environment. Her ambition was now more clearly defined: to be the best she could be for God in that role.

Questions

1. What are your experiences of good and bad ambition in your work environment?
2. What role models for godly ambition do we find in the Bible?
3. In what ways do your ambitions either align, or conflict, with your professed Christian faith?

4. Competition

'The trouble with the rat race is that even when you win, you're still a rat' LILY TOMLIN

Is competition God–given, and therefore fundamentally good? Or is it a result of the fall and therefore fundamentally bad, or somewhere in-between? To what extent are you motivated by your competitive instincts at work? Like ambition, competitiveness can be a very positive Christian quality when it channels the drive to fulfil our God-given potential to be creative, to serve, to step out in faith. It can also turn ugly when it leads to self-obsession, self-aggrandisement and self-promotion.

I have never heard a talk in a Christian context about competition. Is it that it is not important, or is it something we don't want to talk about in church settings? … I suspect the latter.

Competition is closely linked with the desire to get ahead (Chap. 2), and ambition to succeed (Chap. 3). If you are ambitious, then you probably have a strongly competitive instinct. Where does that come from and what role, if any, does it have in Christian character and behaviour?

Evolutionists might say it comes from the primeval jungle where we had to compete to survive. It's part of our DNA; an inbuilt response. 'If you threaten my turf, my possessions or my self-respect, then I will protect my position.' It is certainly part of our human-ness.

Competition starts to show itself from an early age. Children learn to compete in family games, they compete for attention; they compete in the playground for friends and for the approval of their teachers and parents. In teen years, the game changes as young people compete in exams, in sport and for the acceptance of their peers.

In any competition, by definition, there are always winners and losers. Most of us have to compete to get a job. There may be over a hundred applicants for one position. One 'wins' and ninety-nine 'lose'.

At the Olympic Games, only three people (or teams) get to stand on the podium to receive medals. Only one gets the Gold.

Parents can be very competitive. You only have to watch them at their children's school events to verify that. Typically, they really want their child to *win;* to have the best role in the school play, or the best position in the team. We all have different degrees of competitiveness in our character and different ways of expressing it. Some people just can't help being competitive in everything. Our family gets very competitive when we gather at Christmas and start on our favourite card games.

C. S. Lewis exposed the dark side of competition in a penetrating address entitled 'The Inner Ring'.[12] He characterised the inbuilt fear of losing out, of being excluded from the 'in crowd', 'the cool people', 'the decision makers', the 'honoured ones'. It's a fear which can drive the worst kind of competitive behaviour. It's there in the school yard, the sports team, and the office; in business, in college and in politics. Lewis summed it up in these words: 'I believe that in all men's lives at certain periods, and in many men's lives at all periods, is the desire to be inside the local Ring and the terror of being left outside'.

Striving to be included and accepted means we take our eyes off our goal to serve the Lord and one another. I recently heard a University Professor speak about a period in her life when her competitive drive to be accepted in the inner circle of her peers seemed to take over. But it gave her no satisfaction. In that process she said, 'I did not like the person that I was becoming'.

Like ambition, being competitive can be either good or bad. As always, the Bible gives us wise principles and some good examples to keep us on the right track. It reminds us that competitive instincts, like all human characteristics, get spoiled by sin.

Bad competition

Jesus' first disciples were a pretty competitive bunch. Luke describes one ugly scene which made Jesus really angry:

---

12. 'The Inner Ring', C. S. Lewis, Memorial Lecture at King's College, University of London, 1944.

'An argument started among the disciples as to which of them would be the greatest' (Luke 9:46).

Paul got equally angry with the Corinthian church because they were boasting to one another about the status of their respective leaders ... *'I follow Paul ... I follow Apollos ... I follow Cephas'* (1 Cor. 1:12). They were seeking reflected glory, success by association. They had lost sight of the centrality and authority of Jesus as the leader of the Church. Unfortunately, we still see this in some churches today, when its members start to feel a smug pride because their church has got a more famous preacher or worship leader, or has a longer history, a bigger congregation or a better building than the one down the road! Competition intrudes everywhere.

Competition can lead to arrogance, abuse of power and corruption; cutting corners to beat the other guys. It can make us so focused on the outcome (winning), that we lose sight of the people who get hurt along the way. Our competitive instincts can override our desire to treat other people well. A work colleague, who readily admits to being very competitive, put it like this: 'We can easily turn the shovel we use to dig with into a sword we use to fight'. He added 'If I get too outcome focused, I forget the process is important as well'.

Competition gets really nasty when we start to despise our competitors and denigrate the opposition. When we don't mind whether we win so long as our enemy doesn't, or worse, like the character in the Iris Murdoch novel who asserted: 'it is not enough to succeed ... others must fail'.[13]

In a competitive world, we naturally find ourselves comparing ourselves with others. Even the Apostle Paul recognised this temptation: *'We do not dare to classify or compare ourselves with some who commend themselves. When they measure themselves by themselves and compare themselves with themselves, they are not wise'* (2 Cor. 10:12).

A friend of mine put it like this 'When I start to compare myself with other people, I don't feel good about myself'.

---

13. Iris Murdoch, *The Black Prince*, (Chatto and Windus, London, 1973), p. 98.

Good competition

The desire to compete and win in business, and in life, is a powerful motivator.

I have spent my working life in the infrastructure business. Companies compete to win work. They put in long hours preparing their tender. Maybe several firms bid ... only one wins.

You can't succeed in business without being competitive. From a multi-national corporation to a single trader, your product or service has to be higher quality and/or lower cost than the next guy's to be successful. Businesses that cease to be competitive quickly cease to exist!

Competition drives hard work and commitment. It also drives innovation. In the early days of the Covid-19 pandemic, there was intense competition between scientists, institutions and even nations to find an effective vaccine. Competition brings out human courage and endurance; think of the 'race' to reach the South Pole in the early-twentieth century and the race to be the first to climb Everest. Competition develops character. For every winner there are many 'losers' who have to learn to cope with setbacks and develop resilience and persistence to keep going. For anyone involved in professional sport, winning and losing is simply part of the business.

Being authentically Christian in a competitive world can be a testing experience, especially for those with strong competitive instincts.

It is usually impossible to unravel the complex weave of mixed motives that characterise human behaviour. Most of us just want to win! If you are not competitive by nature, then you may have skimmed through these thoughts as of little relevance or interest to you. But don't dismiss too readily those with strong competitive instincts as 'un-Christian'. If we are competitive by nature, let's ask God to channel that in the right direction, so that we always seek to do the best we can for the good of others and not just for ourselves.

What sort of race?

The picture of an athletic race to describe the Christian life is used several times in the New Testament (see for example 1 Corinthians, 2 Timothy, and Hebrews 12). But it's not a picture of a competition, but

rather of finishing the course set before us. In today's culture, it's more like a marathon which, for most amateur runners, is about completing the event and performing a personal best time, rather than winning. Thank God, He doesn't present us with the prospect of a competition for a limited number of slots in heaven! The Christian 'race' is not one where only the best, the most loving, the most self-sufficient the most religious get in. It's not like an entry exam where only the top 5 per cent 'make the cut'. Jesus' ministry in the gospels makes that very clear. He told the Pharisees, and His disciples, that 'the last shall be first and the first last': the popular favourites to be first into heaven (the religious leaders) were, in truth, right at the back, behind the rejects of society who were humble enough to recognise their need of the grace of God.

Jesus said *'Come to me all you who are weary and burdened and I will give you rest'* (Matt. 11:28). This is a wonderful, open invitation, not a ticket for a competition.

Questions

1. How strong are your competitive instincts? How do they manifest themselves?

2. What difference does your Christian faith make to the way you harness and channel those instincts at work?

3. What encouragements and warnings do you find in the Bible about good and bad competition?

5. Rewards

'Each will be rewarded according to their own labour'
(1 Cor. 3:8)

Most of us are motivated by rewards. We instinctively want to know 'What's in it for me?' though we may be reluctant to admit it. The particular reward that motivates us to work may vary according to our personality and our stage in life. Wise leaders understand how to use rewards to motivate their staff. If we insist that we are not *motivated* by rewards, then let's at least admit to being *encouraged* by them.

Praise and recognition are great motivators. Which of us is not encouraged at being thanked, or commended in front of our peers? It's very dis-heartening to receive no thanks, recognition or encouragement. A senior doctor at our local hospital was flat out busy on his rounds. As he passed a cleaner in the corridor, he suddenly felt prompted to stop and thank her for all her hard work. To his great surprise, she burst into tears, and thanked him with these words, 'No one has ever said that to me before!' I may be motivated by the desire to do my job the best I can, but it's still encouraging to get recognition for my efforts. A leading sports coach was asked about how he motivated his players to produce their best. He observed, 'I never saw anyone go backwards through too much encouragement'.

Money of course is a huge motivator. That's why production bonuses, sales incentives and income linked to key performance indicators work in the business world. A friend considering a job offer confided; 'I don't care what title they give me, or whether or not I get a fancy office, just show me the money. How big will my bonus be? That's all I need to know'.

Others are more motivated by status. A former work colleague was considering an offer to move to another organisation. He said, 'I'm not

so concerned about the money, but I've told them that I won't accept the job unless they give me a decent title'.

The more altruistic, but often intangible, reward of helping others flourish is also a big motivator. Parents invest thousands of hours in their children, simply out of love and the desire to see them develop their gifts and fulfil their potential. Committed schoolteachers and carers put in extra hours beyond the call of duty. Those who instruct apprentices in practical skills, or mentor future leaders, enjoy a similar satisfaction which often motivates them to work harder and longer.

I know many people who find their reward *simply from doing their job well* and from the satisfaction and sense of fulfilment to be found in solving a difficult technical, legal or financial problem. I asked Margaret, a nurse and former office worker, what motivated her at work. She replied simply, 'Knowing I've done a good job …. I feel good'.

Sometimes that is sufficient reward in itself.

What did Jesus say about rewards?

Jesus' disciples seemed to be very keen on rewards. They wanted to know what the deal was: '*We have left everything to follow you! What then will there be for us?*' (Matt. 19:27).

They had given up a lot to follow Jesus, or so they thought at the time. What was in it for them? In reply, Jesus promised them that such sacrifice would be rewarded, but not necessarily with material things. The experience of Christians over two millennia is that these rewards are more often spiritual than material. Those who promise material prosperity in this life as a reward for following God are flying in the face of the Bible and badly misleading those who listen to them. The experience of the Apostle Paul was a long way from an attractive picture of material success: '*We are hard pressed on every side, but not crushed; perplexed, but not in despair; persecuted but not abandoned; struck down but not destroyed*' (2 Cor. 4:8-9).

Some of Jesus' parables (such as the parable of the talents in Matthew 25) imply that there are rewards, and different degrees of rewards, in heaven. I find this hard to understand, probably because of the way our innate selfishness distorts our thinking. If you hear that someone else

has received a bigger pay rise than you, or gets the promotion instead of you, don't you get a little envious? But there can't be envy in heaven or else it would cease to be heaven. Therefore, it follows that if there are different rewards in heaven, we won't be worrying about them anyway! Everything will seem fitting and we will be content and fulfilled in the presence of Christ. If we get to heaven, it is by the grace of God not because we have 'earned a reward' (Eph. 2:8-10).

But, the gospels don't play down rewards. For example, in the Sermon on the Mount, Jesus spoke against making a public display of our piety. If we choose to pray, fast and give to the poor, then we should do it privately, not for public show. In each case Jesus promised that, 'Your Father who sees what is done in secret will reward you' (Matt. 6:4).

On another occasion, Jesus promised that those who showed mercy and kindness to the weak and disadvantaged would not lose their reward (Matt. 10:42). Jesus seems to encourage the idea that our heavenly reward is meant to motivate us to serve Christ here on earth, especially in the face of suffering and persecution: *Blessed are you when people insult you, persecute you and falsely say all kinds of evil against you because of me. Rejoice and be glad, because great is your reward in heaven ...*' (Matt. 5:11, 12).

Self-interest—a big test?

The cynic may say, 'never bet against self-interest. It wins every time'. One book on motivation[14] argues that leaders should stop trying to motivate employees with high ideals and focus on their natural selfishness: 'what's in it for them'. It also urges bosses to be real, to stop kidding themselves and realise how selfish they are themselves.

In that sort of competitive secular environment, any resolve we may have to work 'for the Lord', and seek our reward from Him, will be tested. More tangible rewards may well start to look more attractive and dominate our behaviour. But, when our prime motivation for work becomes a desire to earn more money, or win

---

14. Dan Gregory and Tim Flanagan, *Selfish, Scared and Stupid*, (Wiley, 2014).

the accolades of others, or attain a certain status, with its prestige, wealth and respect, then we are likely to end up disappointed. Even if we succeed in gaining the rewards we have craved, we will find they will not satisfy our deepest need. They cannot fill the vacuum in a life where God is excluded or pushed into second place. You might think that this should be obvious to most Christians, but in environments where money and success dominate … it isn't.

We are all wired differently. Thankfully our Creator God knows that even better than we do. If we want to understand ourselves better, then let's ask God (and those close to us if we're brave enough!) to show us our weak points. And let's ask ourselves: 'how does my natural longing for rewards need to be brought into line with the teaching and example of Christ?' It's all part of the process of God probing our motives and changing us by His Holy Spirit through our testing experiences, including those at work.

Questions

1. What forms of rewards motivate you? Money, recognition, appreciation, job title, job satisfaction?

2. In what ways can a natural love of rewards be harnessed for good at work?

6. Contentment or Adventure?

'He was a man of short views, interested in the here and now, the concrete. He left larger goals and claims to others, contenting himself with smaller ones: a happy family, a decent life, the attempt to do his job as well as he could. It seemed to him little enough to ask of life and he settled for these hopes' [15]

These words describe Commissario Brunetti, a fictional detective hero based in Venice; an attractive character, a thinking man, not particularly ambitious or competitive. He wasn't anxious to climb higher up the organisational ladder. Rather he was motivated simply by the desire to do his job, solving crimes, catching criminals, staying one step ahead of his impossible boss and enjoying his family life with long lunches, accompanied by occasional glasses of Prosecco!

When I was in my early teens, I had a schoolmate whose father was a pharmacist. Every evening after returning from work, he would eat dinner and then relax in the lounge room with his wife, reading or watching TV in an atmosphere of quiet companionship. 'How boring!' I thought. Why couldn't he do something more exciting? Later I found out that he had fought in the jungles of south-east Asia in the Second World War. Having survived the war, and some horrific experiences, he wanted no more adventures. His motivation for work was to sustain a quiet, decent life in the relative safety of suburbia. My respect for my friend's father soared. I learned that people are often much more than they seem, and we are best not to be critical.

Those who quietly get on with their daily work with integrity, and with a minimum of fuss, are like the glue which binds any community

---

15. Donna Leon, *A Sea of Troubles* (Arrop Books, 2012), p. 102.

together. But perhaps there are too many of us living in a state of self-absorbed contentment, preferring to fly low under the radar; avoiding trouble, not wanting to make a stand as a Christian, not wanting to speak out in the face of injustice, bullying or harassment; not wanting to rock the boat, needing a wake up call, reluctant to become 'discontents for God'.

The writer of Ecclesiastes emphasises repeatedly[16] that enjoying our work, and finding contentment in that work, is a gracious gift of God (Eccles. 5:19). But the Bible also gives us a very different perspective on 'the quiet life'. We can easily get *too* comfortable in our job, our home and our circle of friends. At such times God may wake us up from our spiritual torpor and call us to take on a new role, to do something that stretches us and tests our faith.

A quiet life disturbed

Moses had been living the quiet life for some forty years. As a brash young man in Egypt, he had stood up against injustice and killed an Egyptian who was beating a Hebrew slave. He had to run for his life. He found a wife, a new community and work as a shepherd out in the desert. As he grew old, he seemed reasonably content and was no doubt working out how to enjoy an easier life in his later years. Then God spoke to him and gave him a really difficult job to do: one of the greatest adventures of faith of all time. His quiet life was over!

The book of Exodus tells us how God sent him back to Egypt with the seemingly impossible task of getting Pharaoh to release all his slaves. Then He gave him an even bigger job, to lead the people of Israel out of Egypt into the 'Promised Land' of Canaan.

How did Moses respond to this unmistakably clear call from God to leave his quiet, ordered life to take on this daunting leadership role? Did he jump in and say 'Right God, I'm ready. I've been wondering why you haven't used me all these years'? No! Perhaps, like us, when God disturbs our quiet, comfortable situation to do something for Him, Moses came up with a series of excuses (Exod. 3:11–4:17). You might be able to identify with some of these.

---

16. See also Ecclesiastes 2:24; 3:13.

Excuse 1: 'I am not up to the job' Moses asked ... 'Who am I ...?' (3:11), i.e., 'I am totally unsuited for this task'. God's answer: 'I will be with you ...' (3:12).

Excuse 2: 'the people don't know about God ...' Suppose I go to the Israelites and say to them, 'The God of your fathers has sent me to you, and they ask me "What is his Name?" Then what shall I tell them?' (3:13). God's answer: 'I AM WHO I AM ...' (v. 14). Moses learned something new ... the holy name of God and His eternal nature and power.

Excuse 3: 'No one will listen to me ...' 'What if they do not believe me or listen to me and say, "The LORD did not appear to you?"' (4:1). God's answer: 'What is that in your hand ...?' (4:2) It was a shepherd's stick, the tool of his trade, what he used every day. Moses made a new discovery: God works with what we have got, and He has total power over His creation.

Excuse 4: 'I don't have the gifts' 'I have never been eloquent ...' (4:10). God's answer: 'Go. I will help you speak and will teach you what to say' (4:12).

Excuse 5: 'Not my problem!' *'Moses said, 'O Lord. Please send someone else'* (4:13). Notice this was real unbelief and disobedience. It came after God had promised to be with him and after He had showed Moses His miraculous power. God's promise: Aaron his brother will go with him to help him (see 4:14-17).

God patiently dealt with each excuse and revealed more of Himself in the process. Don't you find that encouraging? His promises are always enough for us to move forward in faith.

Adventures at work?

Do you think of your daily work as an adventure? Probably not. More likely we think of adventure as what happens at weekends or on holidays.

I love being in the mountains. I used to have a wall poster showing a climber high up in the Himalayas with the caption 'Never stop exploring'. After a frustrating day working and living in a big city, and commuting in heavy traffic, it inspired me to think of places I would like to escape to!

I grew up reading adventure books, true stories of people like Scott and Shackleton, Ibn Battuta, Marco Polo, Muir, Mawson, Amundsen and Shipton. Later in life I was inspired by the adventures of pioneer Christians like Gladys Aylward who exchanged their comfortable lives to serve in really difficult situations. But I have since learned that you don't have to move anywhere to have an adventure. Adventure can be a state of mind.

Perhaps you would love to travel but you can't. You have elderly relatives or children with special needs to look after. You have commitments you can't leave, or you simply don't have the money. Perhaps you have never felt the desire to live or work anywhere else. God may call us to adventures of a different kind: to stay right where we are but do something to make a difference, in our workplace or in our community.

I have also learned that one person's adventure can be another person's routine. What is difficult to one is relatively easy to another. In my thirties, my wife and I, and two young children, moved from the UK to live and work for five years in Papua New Guinea. While we were packing up, a friend was starting a job in a high-crime, inner-city environment in the north of England. He said to us that he couldn't understand how we could move our young family across the world 'just like that' so easily. I stopped and realised that for us it wasn't a problem—we were looking forward very much to the opportunity. We would have found it much more difficult to relocate to the inner-city location that my friend was working in.

Thank God, He equips us all differently for the particular adventure of faith He calls us to, whether at home or overseas. When we first arrived in PNG, an expatriate who had worked there for twenty years, questioned our real motives for being there. He challenged us like this: 'there are three types of expat workers here: missionary, mercenary or mad. Which are you?' I think if we were honest, we were a mix of all three!

Ignatius Loyola, founder of the Jesuits in the sixteenth century encouraged his followers to live 'with one foot raised', to be always ready to go wherever God was calling them. But the issue is not so much *where* we might go, as whether we are prepared to step out of our comfort zone and trust God with our lives.

Questions

1. At what point in your experience does a desire for contentment turn into a self-indulgent love of comfort and an easy life?

2. To what extent do you have a 'do not disturb' notice hanging over your life? How much of what you do is aimed at not rocking the boat, avoiding unwanted interruptions to your plans?

3. Is God wanting to give you a 'wake-up' call, to step out of your comfort zone in faith and do something for someone else, or to stand up for someone else?

7. Pride

'As long as you are proud you cannot know God. A proud man is always looking down on things and people: and of course, as long as you are looking down, you cannot see something that is above you'[17]

Pride—a motivator?

If I described a friend to you by saying, 'she takes great pride in her work', you would know exactly what I meant. I would be paying her a compliment by saying that whatever she did, she gave it her best.

Pride in our work can be a great motivator. I recall, as an eleven-year-old, being told by my school teacher (who in retrospect was probably having a bad day) that I was not good enough to go to the high school I was aiming for. My pride was stung and it was obviously hurtful at the time. But, I also remember how that motivated me to redouble my efforts in passing the entrance exam and proving him wrong!

When the sports coach tells her players who are being hammered by the opposition, to 'have some pride in the jersey', she is appealing to their desire to give their best for the team, even if they lose the game. When our pride is hurt, we often perform better with an 'I'll show them' attitude.

Even when we don't need to prove anything to anyone, most of us take personal pride in turning out the best product that we can or providing the best service we can. If you work for an organisation you respect, you will probably take pride in representing that organisation and being associated with it. It's a good feeling to be proud of your employer, or the 'brand' you represent, and a powerful motivating force.

---

17. C. S. Lewis, *Mere Christianity*, 1952 (Harper Collins, 2001), p. 124.

Pride has been called the deadliest of all sins. Augustine called it 'the beginning of all sin'.[18] So, if pride in our work is good, why is pride such a problem?

Pride—a trap?

Pride definitely falls into the 'temptation' category of our experiences of testing. The Bible warns us that pride in what we possess and boasting about what we have achieved is a feature of life in 'the world', i.e., human society trying to live without God. It also warns us that such pride is empty, because even our best successes don't last.

'Do not love the world or anything in the world. If anyone loves the world, love for the Father is not in them. For everything in the world— the lust of the flesh, the lust of the eyes and the pride of life—comes not from the Father but from the world. The world and its desires pass away but whoever who does the will of God lives forever' (1 John 2:15-17).

At the same time, when we acknowledge that all our gifts, brains and energy come from the God who created us, we don't need to be over-shy about our achievements, but we do need to deflect the glory and honour back to God. The Apostle Paul didn't shrink from reminding people in his letters about what he had achieved, but he added '*... by the grace of God, I am what I am'* (1 Cor. 15:10). This wasn't just a polite qualifier to make him look more humble. Paul meant it. Giving glory to God is not a showy public display which subtly draws *more* attention to ourselves. Rather it is seen in quiet humility and thankfulness.

Pride and boasting go naturally together. Paul warns about boasting of what is actually a gift from God: *'What do you have that you did not receive? And if you did receive it, why do you boast as though you did not?'* (1 Cor. 4:7).

The book of Proverbs warns about boasting about our *plans* and what we want to achieve: *'Do not boast about tomorrow, for you do not know what a day may bring'* (Prov. 27:1). In his New Testament letter, James develops this idea further to warn us against the pride of thinking we have our future plans all under control:

18. Augustine, *'On the Sermon on the Mount,'* trans. William Findlay (1888), Book I, Ch. 1.

'Now listen you who say "Today or tomorrow we will go to this or that city, spend a year there, carry on business and make money". Why, you do not even know what will happen tomorrow. What is your life? You are a mist that appears for a little while and then vanishes. Instead you ought to say, "if it is the Lord's will, we will live and do this or that". As it is, you boast in your arrogant schemes. All such boasting is evil' (James 4:13-16).

As I write this, the global Coronavirus pandemic has frustrated the plans of millions of people. It has reminded us that human life is fragile, that we are not as in control as we like to think. For many of us, having to re-set our expectations is a painful and humbling process.

Pride out of control

The Old Testament Book of Daniel gives us a vivid example of someone whose pride in themselves, their status and accomplishments, got totally out of control. King Nebuchadnezzar, the supreme ruler, looked around at the great riches and power of his Babylonian empire and uttered these unforgettable words: *'Is not this the great Babylon I have built as the royal residence, by my mighty power and for the glory of my majesty?'* (Dan. 4:30).

Note his focus on 'I' *and* 'my'. Perhaps you know people who convey such a sense of their own importance and invulnerability that it blinds them to their own weakness. Their success is all about *them*. Their inflated ego leads them to regard others as lesser beings. Maybe you know some 'mini-Nebuchadnezzars'. Maybe you are one! Very few people handle success well. Sometimes God humbles us with a stark reminder of our mortality and vulnerability, as he did Nebuchadnezzar.

Having pride in our work, and giving it our best, is one thing, being so proud that we belittle the contribution of others and forget that all our skills and energy comes from God is another.

Guarding against pride

We are all tempted to pride, albeit in different ways. So how do we guard against it?

Pride and delusion often go together. If we are 'successful' in our work, we can easily start to believe we are somehow better than other people. How do we avoid falling into that trap? The Bible points the way forward:

- Acknowledging God: *'Humble yourselves therefore under God's mighty hand, that he may lift you up in due time'* (1 Pet. 5:6). If we insist on ignoring God and feeding our ego, then, as a wise friend reminded me, 'God has his own ways of keeping us humble'!

- Surrounding ourselves with people who are not afraid to tell us the truth. If you have a friend, colleague, brother, sister, wife or husband who will help keep your feet on the ground when you start to fly into a fantasy world of believing how great you are, then you are very blessed!

- Remembering that all we have been able to do in this life is because God has enabled us to do it. Turning our self-congratulatory thoughts into thanksgiving to God is a great antidote to pride (Ps. 103:2).

- Keeping our feet on the ground; by treating everyone with respect. If we have a senior position, then let's not demand honour and attention. Let's remember that any position is temporary: we only occupy it for a while, as a steward.

Romans 12 makes this last point repeatedly: *'Do not think of yourself more highly than you ought ...'* (v. 3) *and 'Honour one another above yourselves'* (v. 10) ... *'Do not be proud, but be willing to associate with people of low position. Do not be conceited'* (v. 16).

Questions

1. What achievements in your life are you most proud of? Thank God for each of them. Thank Him for giving you the opportunity, the energy and the skill. Thank Him also for all those people who have helped you along the way.

2. How does 'pride in your work' express itself in your life? How can you glorify God through that?

3. Do you have someone in your inner circle of friends and family who is brave enough to tell you the truth about yourself? If not, why not try to find someone who will?

8. Self-Image

'Many college students do not choose work that actually fits their abilities, talents and capacities, but rather choose work that fits within their limited imagination of how they can boost their own self-image'
TIM KELLER[19]

When my eldest daughter graduated from high school, almost all the high achievers chose to study law, commerce or medicine at university. Many subsequently dropped out in the first year. Why? At that time, only students with the highest grades would be accepted for those courses which were in high demand. So, the very fact that they were offered a place gave them a certain 'standing' among their peers. It was good for their image. But as they got stuck into the routine slog of their coursework, they realised this was not what they really wanted to be doing. Some learned the hard way that this was not the best basis on which to make good life decisions.

Striving for self-fulfilment and self-actualisation through life choices about work is never going to satisfy our deepest needs. Seeking to enhance our image through the course we choose, the type of work we do, or the position of importance we strive for, will inevitably disappoint in the end because it is entirely focused on ourselves.

We may naturally assume that we have the sole right of choice over the way we live and the work we choose to do. As Tony Payne insightfully observes: 'there are very few beliefs that everyone in Western society holds in common these days, but this is one of them: the absolute right to personal determination .... It is the default position of all our minds even of those of us who are Christians. We may know and acknowledge that God is truly God and that we should

---

19. Tim Keller, *Every Good Endeavour* (Hodder & Stoughton, 2012), p. 108.

submit to *his* plans for our lives; yet we underestimate just how far down the roots of self-determination go in our souls'.[20]

The temptation to always put ourselves first is very strong. But the Christian gospel presents a radically different way of thinking and living.

A radical alternative

Jesus promised His followers *'fullness of life'* (John 10:10), but He also made clear that to experience that fulfillment we need to be prepared for self-sacrifice:

> *'... unless a kernel of wheat falls to the ground and dies, it remains only a single seed. But if it dies, it produces many seeds'* (John 12:24).

Jesus highlighted a simple principle of nature. A seed must be buried into the ground if it is to grow. When it grows, that single seed multiplies itself, sixty, eighty or a hundred-fold. He applied this principle to Himself. He was to die as the one sacrifice for the sins of the world so that life would result for millions who put their faith in Him. He then applied the same principle to all who follow Him.

The Apostle Paul understood and experienced this reality when he wrote to the Christians he was sacrificing so much to help: '... *death is at work in us, but life is at work in you'* (2 Cor. 4:12). Paul realised that his suffering and hardship was helping many people come to faith in Christ. Some of Paul's letters in the New Testament were written from prison ... they continue to inspire and challenge millions round the world today. That single seed of his self-sacrificing life has produced a massive harvest.

Whether or not we experience physical suffering for our faith, as Paul did, the principle of dying to produce life applies to every Christian. As the late Festo Kivengere, Bishop of Uganda used to say, 'the cross must cross you'.

The gospel call to 'die to self' is a million miles away from our natural concern for our 'image'; our love of being thought well of by

---

20. Tony Payne, *The Thing Is* (Matthias Media, 2013), pp. 19, 20.

others through our work and achievements. It cuts right across the longing to be admired as we post announcements of our 'successes'—carefully designed to attract the most 'likes'—on our favourite social media platforms!

The Bible has no category called 'cool'. It is not concerned with the image we like to portray. It deals with truth and reality.

Way back in the seventeenth century, Nicolaus Copernicus published his work 'De Revolutionibus Orbum Coelestium' to argue that the sun did not revolve around the earth as was commonly believed, but rather the other way around. The earth revolved around the sun. The gospel requires a similar revolution in our thinking. Understanding that the world centres on God, and therefore we need to get our lives right with Him, is revolutionary and life changing. To realise this is *His* world, that we owe Him worship, and that the world does not centre on us, is humbling.

At the same time the gospel brings us good news of release from a treadmill of working only for ourselves, from a longing to be thought well of and a desire to continually promote our own image. It's not about 'self-improvement' and 'self-realisation'. The gospel calls us to die to self, to acknowledge the rule of Jesus Christ in our lives. As we start to live like that, we discover that the satisfaction and fulfilment we find in our work is more a by-product of living for Christ, rather than a goal in itself.

Questions

1. How much of what I do at work is centred around what others think of me?

2. To what extent does concern about my own image affect my life choices?

3. Why does the New Testament make so much of the importance of 'dying to self' (Col. 3:3)?

PART B
LIVING OUR VALUES

> *'Why do you call me Lord, Lord and do not do what I say?'*
> (Luke 6:46).

It's one thing to profess to hold to Christian values. It's another to live them out. Do we put into practice the commands of Jesus, or do we compromise whenever it suits us? At work, our values will certainly be tested.

You might say you value integrity, but when the opportunity arises to claim more expenses or tax deductions than you are entitled to, or lie to your boss about a mistake, or steal other people's ideas, do you then find yourself acting contrary to that value? If you run your own business, you might claim to value your employees, but do you treat them like a commodity that you buy or sell in a competitive market? Do you hire and fire with barely a second thought about the impact on their lives? If you are on survival wages, do you cut corners, try to get away with doing the minimum and complain to whoever will listen, or do you just get on with your job with a positive attitude?

Part A of this book dealt with motives—'why' we do our work. This Part B is about 'how' we work—the values we bring to our workplace—accountability, faithfulness, service, integrity, our commitment to prayer and witness, and how we sort out our priorities.

If our motivation is the engine which drives us forward, then our values provide the rails along which our engine runs. The way these values are tested in our work, whether through God's 'probing', adverse circumstances or temptation, and how we respond, is the focus of the next few chapters.

9. Accountability

'From everyone who has been given much, much will be demanded; and from the one who has been entrusted with much, much more will be asked' (Luke 12:48).

An option or an obligation?

Accountability can be optional. When I lived in Dubai, walking round the block before work, I would pass a 'Boot camp', a group of people who had chosen to get up before dawn to be shouted at and coerced by their trainer into pushing themselves physically to the limit. They didn't have to do it. They had chosen to make themselves accountable to the group in a desire to shed some kilos and improve their fitness. More serious accountability groups, which help alcoholics and drug and gambling addicts overcome their addiction, work on a similar voluntary basis.

There is a higher level of voluntary accountability when we *choose* to sign a contract which then makes us accountable under law for complying with its terms. For example, if you decide to take out a mortgage to buy a house, you make yourself legally accountable to the bank for making the repayments.

In other areas of life though, accountability is not optional in any sense. Employees are accountable to their employer for getting to work on time, putting in a full shift and not cheating the system. Corporations are accountable to the regulatory authorities for safety and environmental management, and to workplace agreements for paying fair wages and ensuring safe working conditions. Company Boards are accountable to the stockholders. In a democracy, elected representatives are accountable to the people. Every citizen is accountable to the state to pay taxes. Students face accountability in the form of exams. You can miss lectures and ignore the reading material, but eventually you are found out.

If we treat these compulsory accountability areas of life as though they were optional, then we run into problems. Politicians and union officials making fraudulent expense claims, are in the news again as I write this. Perhaps they thought they were above the law or were somehow unaccountable to the people who had elected them. Also making news on a regular basis are businesses caught underpaying their staff and exploiting their casual workers. Their 'mistakes' are now being exposed to public view. Accountability comes with responsibility and demands reliability. If we want a promotion at work, are we ready to carry the greater responsibility and accountability that comes with the pay rise? As the saying goes: 'Be careful what you wish for ... You might just get it'. If your job requires you to sign contracts, certify accounts, sign off on safety procedures, engineering designs or prescribed medication, you know only too well the responsibility you carry. For ships' captains, aircraft pilots, drivers, medical professionals, teachers, company directors and many others, accountability is built into the job.

Sometimes the position we long for entails accountability for the performance of the people under us ... that's tough ... that's the life of the football coach, or the project manager ... if the team does badly, or the project fails, you are the one who gets fired!!

My former boss, when he gathered us together in a room for a planning session, used to say, *'We are the ones we have been waiting for'.*[1] He claimed it was an old American Indian saying but I haven't been able to corroborate that! In other words, if we don't come up with the ideas, no one else is going to do it for us. We're IT! We are accountable!

Whatever our role, at work our accountability to others, is tested. But what about our accountability to God?

A biblical perspective

'... obey your earthly masters with respect and fear and with sincerity of heart just as you would obey Christ ...' (Eph. 6:5).

These words were originally addressed by Paul to slaves, but they underline a timeless principle of accountability to everyone in the

---

1. This phrase was also used as the title of the New York Times bestseller by Alice Walker, Pulitzer prize winner, published in 2006.

workplace. Sure, the worker is accountable to the boss, but bosses are also accountable to treat employees fairly *because 'you know that he who is both their Master and yours is in heaven, and there is no favoritism with him'* (Eph. 6:9).

Jesus' parable of the Good Samaritan (Luke 10) makes clear that we have a general duty of care to our fellow human beings. Indeed, Jesus takes that accountability for helping people to the ultimate level in His parable of the sheep and the goats (Matt. 25). He tells us that those helping the needy are, unwittingly, serving the Lord Himself and those failing to care are effectively spurning the Lord Himself.

We are also accountable to the civic authorities, *'Let everyone be subject to the governing authorities, for there is no authority except that which God has established'* (Rom. 13:1).

Given that accountability is built into every area of human activity, why would we doubt that we are accountable to God for our whole life and every part of it?

Jesus tells us that we are accountable to God for how we use what we have been given: money, time, gifts and opportunities. His famous parable of the talents (Matt. 25) makes that clear. We are accountable for our actions *'For we must all appear before the judgment seat of Christ, so that each of us may receive what is due us for the things done while in the body, whether good or bad'* (2 Cor. 5:10). We are accountable to God even for our words, for everything we have said, good and bad, encouraging or hurtful. Jesus said, *'everyone will have to give account on the day of judgment for every empty word they have spoken'* (Matt. 12:36).

Accountability to one another is part of our accountability to God and accountability to God is not an 'opt-in' arrangement. According to the Bible, there will be no part of our life for which we will not be called to give account to Him.

Accountability in action

After his conversion, the Apostle Paul knew he had been entrusted by God with the specific task of spreading the good news of Jesus Christ. Looking back, he expressed his sense of accountability like this:

- 'I have fully proclaimed the gospel of Christ' (Rom. 15:17-19).

- 'I was not disobedient to the heavenly vision' (Acts 26:19).

- 'I have been faithful' (Acts 20:18-21).

- 'I have fought the good fight, I have kept the faith, I have run the race' (2 Tim. 4:7).

How would you apply the principles of accountability implicit in Paul's' words to express your accountability at work? Maybe something like this:

- 'I aim to do my job the best I can and bring my best thinking, skills and effort to my work as though I were doing it for the Lord Himself';

- 'I aim to help my students, patients, shareholders, bosses and customers even when I don't like them';

- 'I try to value everyone I work with and to treat them as people, not just as a resource to exploit';

- 'I try to build relationships of trust and to look out for my workmates, pray for them and take opportunities to share the good news of Jesus Christ with them';

- 'I have set myself to run the race that God has set before me'.

Of course, we may well fail to live up to commitments like these. That's part of our experience of work as a 'proving ground'. But thank God, as we acknowledge our accountability to Him in all things, we get the basics right and we have His forgiveness when we fail and His promise of a new start each day.

Questions

1. How does your accountability to God affect the way you live and work? What difference does it make to your life, day to day?

2. Who are you accountable to—at work and at home? How does your Christian faith affect that accountability?

10. Faithfulness

'A faithful person who can find?' (Prov. 20:6)

A rare and precious quality

Faithfulness is a rare and precious quality. How does it work out in practice?

It means keeping our word

'The one who ... keeps his oath even when it hurts ... will never be shaken' (Ps. 15:4, 5). This test of faithfulness is a real proving ground for our faith. One of the qualities we usually value highly in other people is that they do what they have said they will do. People who keep appointments and commitments, even when it isn't convenient, even when it costs, whatever their status and role, are worthy of great respect.

A young engineer, being interviewed for a job, said to me very directly, 'You will find that I will deliver what I promise to deliver and when I promise to deliver it'. He got the job and proved true to his words. That sort of faithfulness is a great quality in any workplace. It needs to be recognised and rewarded.

It involves carrying out our responsibilities

You may have a job in which faithfulness in carrying out your task is life-critical. Fixing the machine, treating the patient, looking after the children, or checking safety on the building site may be a life-or-death responsibility. But in any workplace, there are those who take personal responsibility for getting done the routine jobs, whether it's turning off the lights, stacking the chairs or locking up after the meeting. Those who put their hand up and say, 'I'll do that', rather than hiding behind a committee or saying '... not my job, not my problem'; those who take every reasonable care to do the right thing without being afraid of failure: such people, at any level in any organisation, are like gold.

It means working wholeheartedly

To work faithfully is to do the best we can because we are accountable to God and to our employers and workmates. It means we don't freeload, getting someone else to do the 'heavy lifting'. We don't slipstream behind others, trying to get them to do all the work so we can take all the credit.

It means valuing people

Faithfulness flows out of love and self-giving which leads us to deal fairly and honestly with people above, alongside and below us in the hierarchy. We don't let people down. We watch out for them.

But doesn't all this amount to just 'doing the right thing'? Aren't these qualities of responsibility, reliability and faithfulness ones we would expect to see from any well-intentioned person whatever their beliefs? Yes! But the Bible shows us that these qualities are also facets of the character of God, as revealed in our Lord Jesus Christ. They are therefore behaviours that God works to produce in us. They are certainly behaviours that non-Christians expect to see in us.

God's faithfulness

God is faithful. It's at the core of His character revealed to us in the Bible. He keeps His promises. He sticks with us even when we mess up and fail. He is committed to a covenant relationship with us. He will fulfil His purpose in and through us.

The faith of the writer of the book of Lamentations was being tested through stressful and painful experiences, but in those experiences, he was reassured of God's love and faithfulness. He wrote: *'Because of the LORD's great love we are not consumed, for his compassions never fail. They are new every morning. Great is your faithfulness'* (Lam. 3:22, 23).

Jesus is our model for faithfulness. He lived a totally faithful life. He took personal responsibility for doing something that no other human being could do; to reveal God to us in His words, actions and character; to die for the sins of the world and so fulfil His role as our Mediator and Saviour. He was faithful in seeing through to the end what He had been sent to do. On the night before His death, Jesus prayed to His Father, *'I have brought you glory on earth by finishing*

the work you gave me to do' (John 17:4). He did not give up or just go half-way. He went all the way to the cross.

Jesus was totally faithful to His team … *'Having loved his own who were in the world he loved them to the end'* (John 13:1). By contrast, His disciples proved to be totally unfaithful to Him. One betrayed Him (Matt. 26:14-16); one denied Him (Luke 24:62); the rest fell asleep (Luke 22:45, 46) when He needed them most; and finally, when the crunch time came, and Jesus was arrested: *'they all deserted him and fled'* (Matt. 26:56). And yet … Jesus knew that would happen. He forgave them and restored them and continued to be faithful to them, as He is for us today.

As a human being, Jesus embodied faithfulness. He lived and worked on this earth focused on honouring His Father in everything He did and said. If He is our role model, we won't go far wrong.

But He is much more than just an example to follow. He has given us His Holy Spirit to change us. One of the fruits He produces in our lives is faithfulness (Gal. 5:22).

Faithfulness in action

Let me share here two life lessons I have learned about practical faithfulness in the care of people at work.

1. The infrastructure company I worked for sometimes operated in difficult and dangerous parts of the world. At one meeting we were discussing whether we should target work in a war-ravaged country which was particularly dangerous at the time. The conversation ended when our boss said simply, 'We are not going to send our people there'. Notice the words he used. He was showing not only a duty of care, and wise risk management, but a sense of identification with the employees concerned. *'We* are not going to send *our* people …' I learned from him a valuable lesson in responsible decision making.

2. We were working late in the office to meet a project deadline, sustained on adrenalin, pizza and caffeine. About 9pm, one young woman left to go home but came running back into the office a few minutes later in some distress. She had been threatened physically by a man loitering in the car park. Naturally she was shaken and frightened. We realised that we had to do things differently. From then on, when we worked late, we set up a system of accompanying

people to their cars and providing taxi vouchers rather than expecting people to travel home alone at night on the bus or train. This is all very basic stuff, but it was another valuable learning experience for me in what acting faithfully, by taking responsibility for people, looks like in the workplace.

To act faithfully, responsibly, and reliably is simply part of living out Jesus' command to love God and love our neighbour and so show something of the character of God in our life.

Questions

1. What role models do you have of 'faithful people'?

2. What responsibilities do you carry at work? What does it mean in practice to carry these out reliably and faithfully?

3. What people do you encounter in your work? What does it mean in practice to deal faithfully with them?

11. Service

'... even the Son of Man did not come to be served but to serve ....'
(Mark 10:45).

Service is a core Christian value. If we claim to be Christians, then we will want to serve others. Why? Because service is a part of the character of God revealed in Jesus Christ.

My friend Paul Draper has spent the last forty years working on the Indian Ocean Islands of Mauritius and Rodriguez. He has not made a pile of money, nor has he sought status, though his work was recognised by the Mauritian Government, and also by the UK Government, with the award of an MBE.

He went out to Mauritius in 1974 because of his strong affinity with the people, which he had established with Mauritians living in the UK, and because he had a desire to help people. He began by founding a small craft business, employing workers with disabilities who could not get work elsewhere. Once this new venture was established, he moved over to the nearby island of Rodriguez to start again from scratch. He set up a craft business and a beekeeping business, both employing only disabled people who might not otherwise have found work. He also established a school for children with special needs. His entrepreneurial skills have been channelled into building these successful not-for-profit ventures rather than making money for himself. His working life has been spent in service.

You may know people like my friend Paul who work selflessly for other people out of a desire to serve. The world would be a poorer place without them. But what about those who work in more 'normal' paid jobs or work full time in the home? What does service mean for them?

Learning to serve

Most of us learn about service growing up at home, as we help by washing the dishes, cleaning up the backyard or ironing the clothes. Every homemaker is, by definition, a servant; and all for no pay!

My friend Andrew Laird had been talking to his four-year-old daughter about the value of work. Her father went to work, and her mother now worked in the home. But the little girl thought that she herself didn't do any work at all. So, he asked her, 'what is it then when Mum asks you to tidy your room or clear the dishes?' 'That's not work', she replied, 'that's just helping people'. We sometimes learn a lot from our children!

The value of service is widely recognised in the non-Christian world. We rely on volunteer workers, as well as paid employees, to help in hospitals, bring meals to old people, help street kids, advise people on their basic legal rights and do a myriad of other unglamorous jobs. Most societies, and all churches and charities, would quickly grind to a halt without people being motivated by a desire to serve.

Servant—an honoured title

In the Bible we find that God rates service very highly. The Messiah Himself, is described in the Old Testament as 'the Servant of the Lord'.[2] Alec Motyer helpfully sums up the meaning and use of this title like this: *'The Old Testament uses "servant" to describe the relation of the Lord's people to the Lord (Ps. 19:11, 12). Individuals describe themselves in this way (e.g. Moses, Exod. 4:10; Joshua, Exod. 5:14; David, 2 Sam 7:19) ... and are so described by others (e.g. Moses, Exod.14:31; Abraham, Exod. 32:13; David, 1 Kings. 8:24). The title "Servant of the Lord" is used of Moses twenty one times and twice of Joshua. The Lord speaks of "my servant" meaning the people of Israel (e.g. Lev. 25:42) fourteen times including seven in Isa. 40-55. He also refers in this way to Moses (six times, e.g. Num. 12:7), David (twenty one times, e.g. 2 Sam. 3:18) the prophets (nine times e.g. 2 Kings 9:7), Job (seven times, e.g. Job. 1:8) and Nebuchadnezzar (twice, e.g. Jer. 27:6).'*[3]

---

2. Particularly in Isaiah. See for example chapter 42, vv. 1-4.
3. Alec Motyer, *The prophecy of Isaiah* (IVP, 1993), p. 319.

In the New Testament, we find that Jesus set the pattern. He told His followers, '*I am among you as one who serves*' (Luke 22:27). He gave His time and energy for others. He healed the sick and fed the hungry. He washed His disciples' feet to make the point. Finally, He laid down His life. Jesus modelled servant leadership. The Apostle Paul pointed to this example of Jesus as a pattern for every Christian to follow with these words: '*In your relationships with one another, have the same mindset as Christ Jesus: Who being in very nature God, did not consider equality with God something to be used to his own advantage; rather he made himself nothing, by taking the very nature of a servant, being made in human likeness, And being found in appearance as a man, he humbled himself by becoming obedient to death—even death on a cross!*' (Phil. 2:5-8).

This is a very high ideal. But it challenges us to ask ourselves 'how much is my attitude one of service?' If the motto of this world is 'I grab', the motto of the Christian should surely be 'I serve'. We are to serve Christ and to serve one another.

By definition, a servant works so that others benefit. Every job, whether at home, in business, industry, academia, the military or the arts, provides opportunities for service both in the nature of the task itself and in the way we perform it. Andrew Scipione the former Commissioner of Police for New South Wales said, '*The best way I can lead my organisation is to serve them. To enable them to be the best they can be. The best way I can serve the Lord in this role is to serve people, the officers in the force and the people of NSW for whose safety I am responsible. You ask me where I got my leadership style from. I got it straight from the Bible.*'[4]

Every day presents opportunities to serve one another in much smaller ways, to be the one who gets the coffees, the one who actually *does* wash up their own cups and plates, the one who sweeps up the workshop, the one who gives a lift home to someone (other than just a close friend) who is waiting in the rain for the bus.

Tim Keller earths this concept of service at work like this:

'*We are to see work as a way of service to God and our neighbor, and so we should both choose and conduct our work in*

---

4. Speaking at Belgrave Heights Men's Convention, Victoria, May 2015.

accordance with that purpose ... "How with my existing abilities and opportunities, can I be of greatest service to other people, knowing what I do of God's will and human need?"[5]

It's been my experience that people who live out this mindset are usually more interesting and attractive people (in personality) than those who are all out for themselves. It's a living demonstration of Jesus' teaching that the more we try to hold on to things, the more we will lose; the more we give, the more we gain.

Questions

1. Think of people you know who live out Christ's call to serve. In what ways is this demonstrated in their lives?

2. What opportunities are there in your daily work to serve people by 'going the extra mile'?

3. In what way is your daily work itself an act of service?

5. Keller, p. 67.

12. Dealing with Corruption

'The possession of money in this world is a test run for eternity. Can you pass the Luke 16:11 test of faithfulness with your money?'[6] JOHN PIPER

'Our government is corrupt. Business is corrupt. The judiciary is corrupt, and the press is in the pocket of the government. What hope is there?' These words were spoken by a national of a country which was struggling with this huge issue. You can sense her frustration at the way corruption had spread like a cancer through the body. Despite regular anti-corruption campaigns announced by politicians and international agencies, and occasional trials and convictions of leading figures, it seemed impossible to root out corruption from the society.

Transparency International has, for many years, published its Corruption Perception Index (CPI), an assessment of the perceived levels of corruption in countries around the world. The CPI ranks countries according to their level of corruption, on a scale of 1 (most corrupt) to 100 (least corrupt). Countries like New Zealand, Denmark and Singapore consistently rank well as the least corrupt. War-ravaged countries like Syria, South Sudan and Somalia usually rate among the most corrupt.

I wonder, if there was an index measuring the level of corruption in the organisation you work for, how would it rate? If there was a similar independent assessment of the level of corruption of individuals, how do you think you would score? Most of us would probably claim to score well, but does that bear scrutiny? We can get very selective in our judgment at this point. 'Corruption is what happens in other places.' Right? No! Corruption happens almost everywhere. It just takes on different forms.

---

6. https://www.desiringgod.org/messages/preparing-to-receive-christ-hearing-moses-and-the-prophets

I first experienced small-scale corruption as a student, working in a tyre depot. There was a toxic 'us against them' culture, workers versus management. It wasn't helped by the management introducing 'workplace efficiency audits' (known then as 'time and motion studies'), which the workers rightly suspected was a tool for management to decide how they could reduce the workforce in order to lower operating costs. With this hidden threat of losing their jobs, the workers' strategy was obvious: to fill in the forms incorrectly and generally to frustrate and mislead the management as far as possible. If this was a test of my ethics, then I confess to have failed. I joined in with all the workers in the struggle! Dishonest practices seemed to be the norm. Tyres went missing, deliveries to depots were incomplete. There were kickbacks, nods and winks, a 'don't ask, don't tell' culture of worker solidarity. It was a serious 'game' of workers versus the bosses and both sides looked to score points however they could.

At that time I was not a Christian. Looking back, I wonder what difference a Christian faith might have made to the way I acted in that work situation. Would I have had the courage to work and act more ethically? I like to think so, but I don't know. Reflecting on that and other formative experiences of work, I have learned that it is easy to talk and write about ethical standards from a comfortable office, with a regular pay check and a secure job in a relatively peaceful location. Those beliefs are pressure tested and 'proved' when we need money to survive.

At one end of the corruption spectrum are government ministers taking large bribes to award contracts and business concessions to those who will pay the most. At the other end is widespread minor corruption, where some under-the-counter cash payment is required by public officials, to approve immigration permits or to clear imported goods through Customs. A former colleague, whose work took him through several African countries, described the time he was stripped down to his underwear and held for nine hours because the border guards wanted a bribe, which he steadfastly refused to offer.

I once worked for a public sector authority where the two top leaders went to jail for corruption. They were running a scam in which the authority bought houses for its senior staff at artificially high prices with a kick-back side arrangement to share the 'super profit' from the sale with the sellers who 'just happened' to be friends of the bosses.

In western countries, corruption may take more subtle forms: the politicians holidaying on the yacht of the media magnate to get favourable press coverage; the super-wealthy industrialist who wants to influence government policy decisions on the environment; or the mayor who awards the property development rights to his golfing mates in exchange for their financial support of his re-election campaign.

Culture plays a big part in the way corrupt practices are perceived. For example, clan loyalty ranks higher than impartiality on the ethical priority list in some societies. To give a job or contract to a relative is contrary to the rules and ethics of most western organisations. But in some cultures it may be seen as 'doing the right thing', by looking after family.

Corruption is a reality in business and political life everywhere. It just takes different forms. Let's beware we don't condemn it in others while condoning it ourselves. When and how can we make a stand? The Bible gives us some great role models.

Daniel: a stand against corruption

Daniel was an exiled Jew, serving the foreign power that had taken him and other key Jewish leaders into captivity in Babylon. They were on a three-year course, like management trainees, being initiated into the Babylonian culture to serve the king (Dan. 1:1-5). Daniel had rapidly been promoted through his God-given ability to interpret the king's dream and to give wise advice (Dan. 2). Years later, when Darius took over as king, Daniel was appointed as one of the top three managers in the public service. He would have had to handle large sums of money and manage a lot of people. When the king realised his unique qualities and promoted him to be the sole head of the service, jealousy kicked-in and Daniel's peers and underlings plotted together to 'dig up some dirt' on him. They couldn't find any 'because he was trustworthy and neither corrupt nor negligent' (Dan. 6:4).

As a leader in a very responsible position, Daniel stood against corruption in both his personal and public life. He put his faith in a just, righteous God on the line. He was in a religious and cultural minority and he suffered for it, but in the end he was vindicated. When

his enemies tried to get Daniel executed through attacking his faith in God and arguing to the king that this amounted to treason, their plan spectacularly backfired (Dan. 6).

New Testament Christians

In the New Testament, we find the Apostle Peter addressing Christians as 'strangers in the world', people whose true home is now in heaven and who live out their lives on this earth as 'exiles'. How should they live? They should live as good citizens and pay their dues while holding firm to their faith. They should follow Jesus' instruction to *'give back to Caesar what is Caesar's and to God what is God's'* (Matt. 22:21). Peter encourages them:

'Live such good lives among the pagans that though they accuse you of doing wrong, they may see your good deeds and glorify God on the day he visits us ... Live as free people but do not use your freedom as a cover-up for evil. Show proper respect for everyone. Love the family of believers, fear God, honour the Emperor' (1 Pet. 2:12, 16, 17).

The Christian is called to live with integrity in this world. That will come at a cost. The Bible goes on to say that if we are to suffer, let it be for making our stand for Christ and for the integrity He calls for, not for being corrupt.

Corruption in governments and businesses is like rust in a car. You don't wake up one day and find your car has rusted out. It's a slow imperceptible process and we have to guard against it every day. I think that same principle applies to any organisation and to any individual. Perhaps we need to examine our own lives for signs of this kind of 'rust'.

Questions

1. If you were subject to the sort of scrutiny of your personal life and business dealings that Daniel (like many leaders in public life today) had to endure, how would you measure up?

2. What honesty tests do you face in your daily life? How do you equip yourself to face these tests? Read Proverbs 4:20-27.

3. What can you do to stand against corruption in your culture and in your workplace?

13. Living with Integrity

'A person of integrity is moral in their character, principled in action, truthful in dealings, and accountable at all times'[7]

'Integrity is the quality of integrated persons, in whom there is no dichotomy between their public and private lives, between what they profess and what they practice, between their words and their deeds'[8]

With these two definitions of integrity, would you claim to be a person of integrity? In this life, we will never lack opportunities to prove the truth of that claim.

Tests of integrity

I was travelling by plane from Brisbane to Sydney. Relaxing into my seat I noticed an official looking folder in the seat pocket in front. The label on the cover told me it contained the confidential Board Papers for a major company. They had been left there by mistake by a director on the previous flight. It was a company I was interested in, and I had a great desire to read what was inside. I thought of myself as a person with reasonable integrity, so I was surprised at the intensity of the moral battle that started waging in my head. Would I like someone to read my private papers if I had left them on a plane? No! That seemed to settle it. But then another little voice started up. 'Perhaps I should just take a peek so that I know what was in them when I return them'—the voice of rationalising bad behaviour! 'Perhaps this was a God-given opportunity ...' where did that thought come from?! Happily, that little battle of integrity was won. I resisted temptation and returned the papers to a very thankful Board member when I arrived in Sydney. I could of course have shared with you some integrity tests I have failed, but that would be too embarrassing!

---

7. Lausanne Global Integrity Network https://www.globalintegritynetwork.org/
8. John Stott quoted in Foreword of *Integrity*, Jonathan Lamb, (IVP, 2006).

All of us face choices every day, which test our integrity, whether in big ethical decisions in business or politics, or in simple tests of honesty when you steal other people's ideas and claim them as yours; or, when the shopkeeper undercharges you in error; or when you find something of value left on the plane!

It's an encouraging sign that integrity is highly valued by many corporations and individuals, Christian or non-Christian. The Ethisphere Institute publishes a list each year of the 'World's Most Ethical Companies', judged by a panel of eminent individuals. Most businesses would claim to value integrity in their employees and in their business practices. Ethical business is good business. You don't need to be corrupt to prosper.

Of course, it's one thing to claim to value integrity, it's another to act with integrity and to do it consistently. It's estimated that about 80 per cent of the institutions that sold and promoted sub-prime 'toxic' mortgages in the USA prior to the 2008 global financial crisis listed integrity as a core value.[9] What a sad irony!

Question: If so many organisations claim to value integrity, why do governments have to legislate[10] to enforce it? Why is there a need for government authorities to regulate safety, prices, and trade practices, to prevent companies from exploiting their market power?

Answer: Because it's necessary! Without effective regulatory oversight and intervention, human nature will tend to take the moral shortcut. The 2019 Hayne Report contained these damning conclusions about the financial sector in Australia: *'Entities and individuals acted in the way they did because they could ... Experience shows that conflicts between duty and interest can seldom be managed; self-interest will almost always trump duty.'*[11]

The Bible emphasises the importance and value of integrity, not as a mere side issue in regard to our relationship with God, but central to our professed faith.

---

9. Australian Financial Review, 12 November 2015.

10. E.g. US Foreign Corrupt Practices Act.

11. 'Royal Commission into Misconduct in the Banking, Superannuation and Financial Services Industry' Final report, February 2019.

The Old Testament Book of Proverbs has some wise things to say:

- *'The integrity of the upright guides them, but the unfaithful are destroyed by their duplicity'* (Prov. 11:3)—we wander from the path of integrity at our peril.

- *'Whoever fears the LORD walks uprightly, but those who despise him are devious in their ways'* (14:2). Integrity is a characteristic of someone who fears the Lord. Dishonesty is a mark of those who show by their actions a contemptuous disregard for God, whatever they profess to believe.

- *'The LORD abhors dishonest scales, but accurate weights find favor with him'* (11:1). The way we handle money shows what we really think about God. When we deal honestly, we are honouring Him. When we are dishonest, we are kidding ourselves that we won't be held to account and that there is no God who sees or cares.

When we start to take God's Word seriously, there will be a change for the better in our integrity and honesty. I love the story in Luke's gospel of Jesus' encounter with Zacchaeus, a dishonest tax collector, whose life was radically changed when he met Jesus.

A changed man (Luke 19:1-10)

In Judea, in the first century A.D., tax collectors were widely hated as traitors. They collected money for the mighty Roman Empire whose forces occupied their land. They also had a reputation for being corrupt. So long as they collected the tribute demanded by Rome, then the authorities turned a blind eye to the tax collectors taking more than the amount required and pocketing the difference. Tax collectors could make a lot of money. Zacchaeus was a chief tax collector and very wealthy.

Zacchaeus had climbed up a tree to catch a glimpse of Jesus in the crowd. Jesus stopped and greeted him. Jesus clearly knew who, and what, Zacchaeus was, but He didn't confront him with his corrupt practices as we might have expected. No. Jesus simply invited Himself to Zacchaeus' house, an action which caused the crowds to

criticise Jesus because *'he has gone to be the guest of a sinner'* (19:7). Most of them would never have set foot in the house of a despised tax collector.

Zacchaeus was convicted in his conscience just by the mere presence of Jesus. Immediately, he promised to pay back what he had cheated 'four times the amount' (way above the requirements of the law) and, on top of that, to give half his possessions to the poor (19:8).

This sort of practical restitution is a very big deal. If we are guilty of exploiting people, or of corrupt behaviour, then true repentance involves more than just saying 'sorry' to God and apologising to those we have wronged. It involves making restitution where possible and practical. Living with integrity means we fix things, as much as we can, when we do wrong. No wonder Jesus said to the crowd who heard and saw Zacchaeus' public act of repentance, *'Today salvation has come to this house'* (19:9).

Making restitution

A friend from student days became a Christian in his twenties. After hearing the story of Zacchaeus and his encounter with Jesus, he became very convicted about his practice of stealing books in his student years. He couldn't shake off the feelings of guilt. Eventually he decided it was time to make restitution.

He contacted the bookshop which had been the main target of his repeated thefts. He explained that, as a Christian, his conscience was troubling him and offered to repay with interest the value of the books taken.

To his surprise, he received a reply from the shop-owner, thanking him for his offer, explaining that repayment was no longer necessary and ending, 'May your God bless you for your honesty'.

Making restitution, where it is in our power to do so, is an important part of living with integrity. As King David prayed long ago, *'I know my God that you test the heart and are pleased with integrity'* (1 Chron. 29:17).

Taking a stand

A Christian friend of mine is a sole-trader roofing contractor. He described to me the culture of lying and deceit on the site of the major

building project he worked on. The sub-contractors were lying to the head contractor to cover up their shoddy workmanship. Their attitude: 'this won't last more than five years, but we'll be long gone by then'. Everyone on site was being 'encouraged' to cut corners. My friend told his boss, 'Don't even think of asking me to lie for you'. He had drawn his line in the sand.

In whatever work situation we are in, each of us has to decide where to draw our line.

The psalmist prayed: *'May integrity and uprightness protect me, because my hope, Lord, is in you'* (Ps. 25:21)—a great prayer to take to work with us every day.

Questions

1. Do you need to repent of dishonesty and make restitution?

2. What tests of your honesty do you face in your work? Where do you draw the line and make a stand?

3. Read Luke 16:10-13. What principles of integrity in handling money are made by Jesus?

14. Prayer at Work

'Pray continually' (1 Thess. 5:17); *'Devote yourselves to prayer'* (Col. 4:2).

The first casualty or the first priority?

When life gets busy, prayer is often the first casualty.

How can we 'pray continually' and 'devote ourselves to prayer' when we are flat out working, when our minds are preoccupied with the tasks at hand and the people we have to deal with? What role should prayer have in our working day?

Prayer is the way we communicate with God. It takes many forms; spoken words, silent prayers and deep groanings of the heart, when words just won't come (Rom. 8:26). It includes worship, thanksgiving, and meditation as well as asking God for help. Millions of Christians would testify to the reality of experiencing God in times of prayer, whether alone or in a group, in a home, in a church or outdoors, whether using formal prayers or just speaking from the heart.

Prayer, at its best, deepens our relationship with God. It is more than just asking God to do stuff, or reciting words from a book. Jesus made this clear when He taught His disciples how to pray using 'the Lord's Prayer' as a guide. In saying, *'Our Father in heaven, hallowed be your name'* (Matt. 6:9), we affirm that the transcendent Holy God is also, by grace, our Father. In praying *'your kingdom come, your will be done ...'* (v. 10), we ask that heaven's rule will be established in all the mess in this world, as well as in our own lives. In asking God to meet our needs: daily food, forgiveness, guidance and deliverance from evil (11-13) we are expressing our dependence on Him.

When I am away from home on a work trip, I like to call my wife first thing in the morning. Just to hear her voice as we exchange news, talk and pray about the coming day, re-affirms our relationship. When

I put the phone down, I feel better equipped to meet the demands of work. So, when we begin each day by talking to God in prayer, and asking Him to speak to us as we read the Bible, we re-affirm our relationship with Him and are strengthened to meet whatever God has in store for us that day.

Praying experiences

If you feel that work pressure has squeezed out any time for prayer, then why not:

- **use your 'down time' more creatively:** The Bible encourages us to *'pray in the Spirit on all occasions with all kinds of prayers and requests'* (Eph. 6:18). If we are doing a tedious job, or sitting on the bus or stuck in a traffic jam, then why not use that time to pray? I was talking to a friend about this recently and he volunteered, 'I like to pray when I'm driving'. His wife overheard and chipped in, 'I like to pray when he's driving too!' Enough said!

- **find a friend to pray with:** I sometimes meet up with a colleague in the city. 'Shall we go for a coffee?' I ask. 'No, let's go for a walk in the park instead.' So, as we walk, we talk. Then we stop somewhere quiet and pray for a few moments. We both value that half hour in a busy day.

- **pray for others:** On some occasions I have offered to pray with non-Christian friends who are going through a hard time. I don't think I have ever had that offer turned down.

- **make time to pray by ourselves:** I used to enjoy playing basketball and still like to watch big games. Like gridiron and netball, but unlike soccer and rugby, the coach can call a time out in the middle of the game … a time for the team to reset and refocus on the game plan. The gospels tell us how Jesus made a practice of having personal 'time outs', going away by Himself to pray (Luke 5:16). If He needed to do that, how much more do we?

- **pray while we work:** How? Short arrow prayers to God before we go into an important meeting or make a difficult phone call.

Nehemiah prayed for wisdom when his boss put him on the spot, 'The King said to me: "What is it you want?" Then I prayed to the God of heaven and I answered ...' (Neh. 2:4, 5).

- **Pray for those in your church grappling with issues at work:** If you belong to a church or home group, make some time to pray in those settings for people at work.

The Bible encourages us to pray about everything (Phil. 4:6), for example, for:

- God to work in the lives of those we work with (Eph. 1:17).

- wisdom, as we deal with difficult situations and as we type our documents, emails, blogs and tweets (Prov. 3:5,6).

- forgiveness when we mess up (1 John 1:9).

- guidance in making decisions ... remember how Jesus prayed before choosing His twelve followers (Luke 6:12,13).

- success in our endeavours (Neh. 1:11): However clever, skilled, educated or experienced we think we are, it is good to express our dependence on God for giving us all these things and for life itself. It is good to remind ourselves that God is Sovereign in His world and that we need His guidance and help.

- those in authority (1 Tim. 2:1-3).

We can also pray over the problems we face at work. Bob was a maintenance manager for a major manufacturer. He entered the workforce straight from school with no qualifications. I asked him how he had grown and progressed over his working life. He answered immediately: 'I prayed. I prayed for the people, and I saw the factory manager become a Christian. Later, while he was dying of cancer, he phoned me and told me he had only a week to live. Would I come to visit? Of course! I went and prayed with him. I prayed over the technical problems I had to fix and I began to discover that God had given me an understanding of how the machinery functioned. I was able to diagnose and repair problems quite quickly and more efficiently than those with more qualifications than me. I prayed for the organisation ... I just prayed about everything and God answered prayer!'

It took me a long while to realise that I needed to pray for the organisation I worked for. Visiting London on a work trip, I joined a breakfast at a church which included several people who worked for the BBC, Britain's national broadcaster. The organisation was having a bad run. Various issues had made the front page of the national daily newspapers. At the breakfast, we prayed for the BBC as an organisation, as well as for the people who worked there. It was a reminder to me that God cared about the organisation as well as people.

The Apostle Paul lived a pretty traumatic life. He wrote this reminder to pray 'in every situation' from a prison cell: *'Do not be anxious about anything, but in every situation, by prayer and petition, with thanksgiving, present your requests to God. And the peace of God, which transcends all understanding, will guard your hearts and your minds in Christ Jesus'* (Phil. 4:6-7).

What a great promise! Jesus taught His followers to always pray and not give up (Luke.18:1). That's the bottom line here. Let's keep on praying. As we do, we can confidently expect God to work:

> *'I remain confident of this; I will see the goodness of the Lord in the land of the living'* (Ps. 27:13).

Questions

1. Who are you praying for at your workplace?

2. What are you asking God to do in your own life, in your home and in any organisation you are part of?

15. A Witness to What?

'There's someone who takes Christ on the job with him'

Those words were spoken by a workmate about Bert, an electrician working for a government military installation, a man who unknowingly left me the legacy of a great example of living out Christian values. You might want to question the theology of that statement. Did he take Christ to work or did Christ take him? Either way, we get the picture. He consistently and reliably lived the values he professed to hold. He was a living witness to Christ. His workmates saw his faith in action.

I have also met professing Christians who have had the opposite effect. It's very depressing to hear a non-Christian say of a workmate, 'I can't believe that guy calls himself a Christian, the way he treats people'. It's all too easy to succumb to the temptation to divide our lives into separate compartments, to speak and behave one way at church and another at work, one way with our Christian friends and another with non-Christians. This sort of hypocrisy, where we are like an actor playing two roles at the same time, puts a great strain on us because we are dividing into parts what God intends to be whole. God calls us to be one person, to live an integrated life in which our faith is not just a 'religious bit' tacked on, but the foundation for the whole of our life, including our 'working life'.

Ready to say something?

Most of us know what it is like to be put on the spot by our workmates and sometimes to be caught 'off-guard' in conversations in coffee room chat. Perhaps you have been faced with moments when you have a split-second decision: should you speak about your faith or keep quiet? How do you react when you face questions like:

'What did you do on Sunday?', or general comments like:
'Jo's husband is dying of cancer. How can anyone believe in a good God who allows that sort of suffering?'; or
'Religious people are all just hypocrites. Just look at all the child abuse at Christian schools and churches.' Or, the direct challenge ...
'You're not a Christian, are you?'

How do you respond to situations like that? Perhaps the wisest counsel is simply to be yourself. People understandably are repulsed by false religiosity and pious platitudes. You may have been confronted by Christians, eager to get their points across whether you are interested or not!! People remember *you*, and whether you are interested in *them*. They remember whether you are being real or just playing a role, long after they have forgotten any words you have said.

So when should we speak and when is it best to remain silent? We certainly need wisdom here! As a young friend put it: 'the difficulty is that you don't want to create barriers because we need to build teamwork at work. If I talk about Jesus, people just shut off and start to avoid me'.

In the New Testament, Peter's three-point advice about speaking for Christ in a hostile or apathetic world is timeless. *'But in your hearts, revere Christ as Lord. Always be prepared to give an answer to everyone who asks you to give the reason for the hope that you have. But do this with gentleness and respect'* (1 Pet. 3:15).

Sometimes opportunities 'to give an answer' come at unexpected times. I was taking part in a leadership survey. The first question was 'what are the main drivers in your life?' 'My Christian faith and my family', I replied, expecting that the interviewer would move on quickly to the next question ... after all in a secular business world, who wants to get involved in discussions about religion? To my surprise, she then asked, 'So tell me about your faith and why that is important to you?' So, for fifteen minutes we talked and she shared her own search for meaning in life. An unusual opportunity in an unexpected situation.

I have never been a great evangelist at work in group situations, but I have had many good opportunities, in one-to-one conversations to talk about Christian faith, particularly in the face of bereavement, family trauma, and disappointments. There was Dev, a young Hindu

draftsman. I was giving him a lift home when he started to ask questions about my faith. I had a New Testament in the glove compartment and, for the whole trip home, Dev was reading out various scripture verses as I drove and tried to answer his questions about Jesus Christ. That was the last time I saw him. Next morning when he didn't show for work, I learned that he had died of a heart attack in the night. I can't but think that those minutes in the car were one of God's special times.

Ready to do something?

Christians are called not just to speak but to live in a way which honours God. Jesus said, 'Let your light shine before others that they may see your good deeds and glorify your Father in heaven' (Matt. 5:16). Later, the Apostle Peter, who had clearly learned so much from Jesus, put it like this: 'Live such good lives among the pagans that, though they accuse you of doing wrong, they may see your good deeds and glorify God on the day he visits us' (1 Pet. 2:12). Two examples, from my work experience, of Christians quietly putting this into practice come to mind.

Andrew lost his teenage daughter in a car crash. His wife had a mental breakdown and left him. He was desperately alone. No one at work seemed to want to talk about it for fear of upsetting him. Indeed a note was put round the office advising staff not to raise it with him. But Andrew *badly* needed to speak to someone. Bottling it up was destroying him. A wise Christian colleague ignored the official advice, took him to lunch for a long talk and then put him in touch with a counsellor who gave him a lot of help and support and a reason to go on.

Stephanie was a project manager who suddenly lost her job. It was just before Christmas, the very worst time. A Christian friend not only prayed for her and with her. He found her a new position which enabled her to keep her children at the same school and give her family some stability.

Making a difference

We may sometimes feel lonely and isolated at work. We might be the only Christian in our workplace. Perhaps that is God's purpose for our lives. Driving home one night I was reminded of the obvious point that our city's lighting engineer does not put all the street lights in one

location. They are spread around the city to shine into the darkness. So God may place us in seemingly 'dark places'. Paul reminded the Christians at Philippi, who were being persecuted for their faith, that they were called to *'shine among them like stars in the sky as you hold firmly to the word of life'* (Phil. 2:15,16).

Ben is the only Christian in his workplace. He works in a warehouse for a logistics company. He finds it a difficult work environment and a daily battle. 'The guys treat the apprentices like rubbish. I try to be positive and they respond. They want to eat lunch with me,' he says, 'but most of the old guys are just bitter and sad'. Ben's Christian faith is tested everyday as he tries to live out his values and share his faith.

God has gifted some people to be evangelists. He has called all Christians to be His witnesses (Acts 1:8). We will not be faced with a shortage of opportunities to be witnesses to Jesus, whether by words, our behaviour or our actions.

Sam Jackson, a Christian minister, described a life changing experience he had in realising the potential for the people in his church to reach others in their workplaces:

> Something very simple had a profound impact on me recently. I had finished preaching about work—about making good work—about working as if you were working for Jesus (Col. 3:23, 24). And I asked everyone to stand and to face the place that they would be at that same time (10:57am) tomorrow. Literally 360 degrees—all parts of our city—were 'faced.' But it wasn't that sight that impacted me most of all ... It was the realization that these 250 people would encounter literally thousands of people in the next six days—people who would NEVER set foot in a church building. People who have little to no understanding of Jesus and His gospel. People who don't own bibles. People who don't pray ... or do pray, but to no one in particular. People in desperate situations. People without hope. Literally thousands of people. People who I hoped would come one of these Sundays .... wait a minute!
>
> And as I stood there looking at this 360-degree outlook into our city, I realized I had two options. One: continue with the planning, preparation, and promotion and pray that the crowd

would come. Or two: focus my energy on equipping those who were standing—those who had the relationships with the crowd I longed to draw.[12]

Questions

1. In what ways are you a witness to Christ at work in what you say, how you do your work and how you relate to people?

2. What does God want to change in your life to be a more consistent and effective witness to Him in your daily work?

12. Sam Jackson, Toowoomba Community Baptist Church, posted on Malyon Workplace Facebook site, April 15, 2015 and used here by permission.

16. Setting Priorities

'Seek first his kingdom and his righteousness...' (Matt. 6:33).

Living out our values is a real test.

Every day we make decisions which reveal, consciously or unconsciously, what is important to us. But what happens when our values conflict? We might get so focused on working faithfully, and being accountable, that we squeeze out time with friends, our marriage partner, our children or our local church? Or, are we so committed at church that we rush home from work and leave straight after dinner for yet another meeting, with no time to give to family? What comes first? How do we decide?

Juggling, balance or chaos?

I asked a work colleague recently how he was going. His reply: 'to be honest I'm just juggling balls right now!' He pictured life like a juggling game with too many balls in the air ... work, family, church, money, leisure, plus all the jobs that needed doing at home. He was battling to catch the next problem and deal with it before another one landed.

When we talk about 'work-life balance', we have a different picture in mind: continually adjusting the time and energy we spend on one part of our life at the expense of another. But the term itself is flawed. How can we balance work with life? Isn't work part of life? Are we picturing an existence in which 'real life' begins when we throw down tools at 5.30pm or when we walk out of the office on Friday evening?

Even if we stick with the idea of a balanced life, we find the balancing act is multi-dimensional. For most of us there are too many demands on our time and energy, too many people 'wanting a piece of us'.

When events really get out of control, life can seem more like a depiction of chaos theory with lines, dots and circles everywhere. Help!

We just feel overwhelmed by the demands on our life. We feel close to breakdown or burnout. What to do?

Overworked?

Hard work is one thing. Being consumed by work, flat out, stressed out, crazy busy, is another. I spoke recently to a project director on a mining development. He was working from seven in the morning to ten at night, Monday through Fridays, seven to six on Saturdays and eight to two on Sundays. He collapsed for a long sleep on Sunday afternoons and started the whole cycle again the next day. Sure, he was paid a lot of money, but his family hardly saw him.

A lawyer in Singapore told me that her firm expected her to work 'from eight "til late" most days'. Michael is a line manager in a supermarket chain. His boss told him that he was expected to work 'whatever hours it takes' if he wanted to keep his job.

In Japan, there is a special word in the language for people dying from strokes, heart attacks and breakdowns that this over-busy culture eventually produces: 'Karoshi'. It means death by overwork.

God knows we need rest. He didn't design our human body to work seven days a week on any sustained basis. Glen Davies, former Archbishop of Sydney, comments, 'Rest is not work's enemy. Rest is work's partner'.[13] The Bible underlines the even greater importance of setting aside time to honour God, listen to His Word and have fellowship with His people (the Sabbath principle). Just as we are not meant to operate without rest, so we are not created to live without reference to God (Matt. 4:4).

Talking to a friend about the dangers of becoming work obsessed, he asked, 'What about laziness? Isn't that a problem too?' I have to admit that I haven't met too many really lazy people, but I do know people whose religion is sport, who are obsessed with computer games and for whom leisure time is top priority.

So how do we balance? How do we juggle? How do we avoid an overbusy life degenerating into chaos and breakdown? How do we find the right point for us between two extremes of laziness and overwork

---

13. Speaking at the Lausanne Global workplace Forum, Manila, June 2019.

in our particular situation, at our age, and with our health issues? The answer lies in the decisions we make about what we value most and who, or what, we love most.

A question of value

Financial advisors speak about 'value investing' as a way of making money in the stock market. The Bible speaks a lot about value investing, not in financial terms, but in the whole of our life.

The prophet Isaiah asks: *'Why spend money on what is not bread and your labour on what does not satisfy?'* (Isa. 55:2). I have often been challenged by this question. In just a few words it cuts to the heart of the problem. Am I spending my time and energy on things of little importance? Am I working harder and longer just to acquire more stuff? What lasting satisfaction do I get from my investment of time and effort. Isaiah goes on to remind us that only God can satisfy our deepest needs. Listening to His life-giving Word needs to be our first priority, *'Listen, listen to me, and eat what is good, and you will delight in the richest of fare. Give ear and come to me, listen, that you may live'* (55:2, 3). Notice the promise in Isaiah's words, the result of getting our priorities right is a deep sense of satisfaction and fulfilment.

The priority of love

Jesus said: *'Where your treasure is, there your heart will be also'* (Matt. 6:21). What you value shows what you really love, and who you love. If we don't invest time, energy, prayer and emotional effort in our friendships and our marriage, let's not be surprised if our relationships start to fall apart. Ask yourself:

- What promises have I made to my marriage partner before God? What promises have I made to God at the baptism or dedication of my children?

- How can I plan life and set priorities better to show love to friends and family? For example, by blocking time out in my calendar for birthdays, presentations, sports fixtures, school concerts, visits to elderly or sick relatives … as far ahead as I can.

- Do I really need to take phone calls and read emails while sharing a meal with family or friends? Can't the world survive for thirty minutes without my input?

Sometimes it takes a family crisis, a personal trauma or a major work setback to get us to reassess our priorities and realise what is important to us.

But we can't be too prescriptive here, because we are all wired differently, face different challenges and have different priorities. We each need to work this out for ourselves relying on God's help.

Ordering our lives

When our first child was born, we had a service of thanksgiving and dedication at our local church. We were asked to 'order our lives under God' as the key to our commitment as parents to bring her up. So far as I know, that phrase doesn't come in the Bible, but it's a great summary of how God wants us to live.

We may think in terms of a balanced life, of juggling priorities, or creating order out of chaos, but Scripture gives us a different paradigm. It is to consciously put our whole life, work, leisure, relationships— all of it—under the direction of the Lord Jesus Christ and seek His priorities and direction each day (Matt. 6:33).

We can't keep everyone happy. But we can resolve to put Jesus Christ and His kingdom first. That simplifies life a lot.

Questions

1. What are your priorities for your work? Reflect on some of the motives we considered in chapters 1-8.

2. What changes in your life do you need to make to 'order your life under God'?

3. What relationships has God entrusted to you? How do you make time to grow those relationships?

PART C
TRANSFORMING RELATIONSHIPS

> *'I want to test the sincerity of your love …'* (2 Cor. 8:8)

'I could be a great Christian if it weren't for the impossible people I have to deal with!' I've been guilty of thinking like that on several occasions. When I do, I have to remind myself that I am missing the whole point! After all, the Bible makes clear that we are fooling ourselves if we think we can have a good relationship with God when we can't build relationships with other people:

> *'Whoever claims to love God yet hates a brother or sister is a liar. For whoever does not love their brother and sister, whom they have seen, cannot love God, whom they have not seen'* (1 John 4:20).

I was in my late thirties, working for a big, growing company when I had a 'lightbulb' moment. Keen to grow my career and move up the ladder, I had become very project focused. My role was to get things done, to win contracts and deliver projects. One day I sat at the back of a large staff meeting and looked around. I realised how little I knew these people. I knew very little about their background, their families or the pressures they were facing. I realised that I needed to change. I asked for God's help to build friendships with those I worked with. It was a turning point for me in my thinking about faith and work and particularly in building work relationships that have stood the test of time.

In the next seven chapters we will think about how our Christian faith is tested in our relationships at work:

- How do we exercise authority?
- How do we respond to authority?
- How do we handle bullying and harassment?
- How do we deal with conflict?

- Do we look for someone to blame when things go wrong?
- Do we use people and exploit them or respect them?
- How do we deal with loneliness?

To do our work 'In His Name' means being consistent with the character of Jesus. That means caring for one another and building quality relationships.

17. Being the Boss

'For I myself am a man under authority ...' (Matt. 8:9).

Leadership qualities

'What sort of boss are you?' I was conducting a job interview and had been asking all the questions up to that point when the young woman applying for the post stopped me in my tracks with this very good question. I can't remember how I answered but it certainly made me think. If you have any sort of authority in your workplace, it's a good question to ask yourself.

I recently asked a group of people in their twenties, what were the qualities they most admired in bosses they had worked for. Their answers fell into four categories:

- Clarity: they wanted their boss to give clear direction as to where the organisation was heading and what was expected of them as employees
- Fairness: treating people without favouritism
- Integrity: setting an example of honesty and hard work
- Being there for the team: 'knowing they have got my back' was how one person described it. Knowing that when things went wrong, the boss would take responsibility, rather than duck for cover and blame everyone else.

The last quality was valued particularly highly. As I listened, I started to reflect on examples of bosses and leaders, good and bad, who had made an impact on me.

Leaders: good and bad

In my early twenties I learned a great lesson about leadership and authority from a young African who started quietly and finished well.

I was working as a temporary instructor at an outdoor pursuits centre on the slopes of Mount Kilimanjaro. There were forty boys on the course aged seventeen to eighteen, and I had eight in my group. In the early days of the month-long course, it was the extroverts, the loud, ego-centric ones who flexed their leadership muscle and demanded that the rest of the group listen to them. By the end of the course, after the students had been pushed to their limit, physically and mentally, it was Joseph, a quiet young man from Uganda, the smallest in stature in the group, who emerged as the natural leader. In the early days of the course, he said very little. But when he spoke, they all listened. He grew into a position of authority by virtue of his natural leadership skills and the quality of his character, by his humility and quiet strength. By the end of the course, he was the one the group followed.

I learned a lot from Joseph. I learned that you don't have to be in a *position* of leadership to start exercising leadership. He led by example from the outset; by contributing ideas and by working for the good of the team. As the course progressed, those qualities were increasingly recognised by his peers.

Fast forward some thirty years. I was working in the Middle East. One of the managers would come into the office, shout at everybody, telling them what a terrible job they were doing, and no one seemed particularly surprised. A colleague half-jokingly commented that the way to succeed in that environment was to 'Kiss up and Kick down', i.e., flatter and 'butter-up' all those above you on the ladder and tread down all those beneath you! Jesus made clear what He thinks of that attitude in His parable of the unmerciful servant (Matt. 18:21-35). The man who grovelled to *his* boss for forgiveness of *his* huge debt, but who then demanded immediate payment from a poor guy who owed him a small debt he couldn't pay, 'kissed up' and 'kicked down'!

Over my career in the infrastructure business, I've had the privilege of working round the world in many different cultures, in working for different bosses and being in leadership positions myself. I've learned from good leaders and bad. I have found that our view of what makes a good boss depends partly on our personality and culture.

Some prefer consensual, consultative leaders who listen to, and respect, the opinions of their team before making a decision. Others

find such leaders frustratingly indecisive and prefer 'command and control' leaders who have strong convictions and give clear directions. Of course, at their worst, such leaders can be arrogant, self-obsessed and downright dangerous—like the dictator who came to power after a military coup and proudly announced, 'Our country is standing on the edge of a precipice—but with me as President we are going to take a great step forward'. Oops!

Whatever our preference I have learned that all leaders are flawed, albeit in different ways.

Leadership in the Bible

The Bible has many great examples of leadership, some good and some bad. There is Moses the reluctant leader; Joshua the leader who emerged from his mentor's shadow; David, far from perfect, but still one who inspired his men by his devotion to them; Abigail whose wise and timely initiative to right the wrongs of her foolish husband saved the lives of her whole family; and Nehemiah the wise leader, who planned and prayed and delivered on his plan.

The Bible also gives us examples of flawed leadership. For example, there is Gideon, who God called to a leadership position when he was a young man. Somewhere along the line this humble young guy became a brutal oppressor (Judg. 8:6-21). He looked to God to help him defeat the enemy, but once that had been done, Gideon began to rewrite history and claim the credit. Gideon wanted some of the glory and the honour that was due to God. (8:27). Like King Saul, another example of someone rising rapidly from obscurity to national leadership, he started well, but ended badly. Let's look and learn.

Jesus was a leader par excellence. He made the breathtaking claim that '... *All authority in heaven and on earth has been given to me.*' (Matt. 28:18). Perhaps the most telling and perceptive comment on how Jesus exercised His authority was made by a Roman centurion, whose son Jesus had healed. After asking Jesus to exercise His divine healing power, he said, *'For I myself am a man under authority...'* (Matt. 8:9). As a ranking soldier his authority was delegated. He exercised the authority granted to him by his boss. As he looked at Jesus, he recognised someone with divine authority, but he also saw

a man who was Himself under a higher authority, that of His Father. Jesus' authority was all channelled into doing the will of His Father. He was obedient to that calling, even to death.

In His three years of ministry, Jesus showed perfectly all the attributes of leadership that I have come to most appreciate and admire in leaders. He:

- knew where He was going and motivated others to follow
- was totally honest
- was earthed in the real world and related to ordinary people
- was totally committed to the task He had been given
- took full responsibility and accountability for what He had been sent to do
- always lived for the big picture ... the glory of God ... never for Himself
- cared for His followers. He laid down His life for them and didn't ask them to go where He would not go Himself.

There are many books on leadership out there. Let's not neglect the one book that matters most: the Bible itself. And, if we are entrusted with authority, let's look to the example of Jesus.

One day we will have to give account to God for the way we have exercised the authority granted to us. If we use that power in the workplace, and in the home, as those who are accountable to God, and for the good of those entrusted to our care, then we will be servant leaders and we will follow the model of Jesus. (Read also Phil. 2:5-11.)

Questions

1. What positions of leadership and authority has God entrusted to you at work, at home, in the church, in the community?

2. What sort of leader are you?

3. In what ways do you need to change to exercise your authority more in line with Christ's servant leadership role model?

18. Working for the Boss

'Give to everyone what you owe them ... if respect then respect; if honour, then honour' (Rom. 13:7).

Most work situations will test our attitudes to authority in one way or another. In the last chapter we thought about how we exercise authority. Here we look at the other side of the coin: how we deal with authority ... how we deal with our boss.

For example, how do you behave when you think you can do your boss's job much better than they can? Are you tempted to undermine their authority at every opportunity, either by going over their head to their boss, or by criticising them behind their back to whoever will listen?

Perhaps you have come home sometimes seething with frustration about your boss, their unrealistic expectations, their pedantic fault-finding or their failure to give clear direction. If you work for a big organisation (government or private) you may get frustrated by the bureaucratic procedures, which seem to you so pointless, but which your boss insists on following.

The Bible speaks a lot about respect for authority (Rom. 13) and about submission (e.g. Eph. 5:21). But this raises the question: when and how should we assert ourselves and stand up for our rights?

Asserting our rights

When I get the opportunity to visit another workplace, I am always interested to scan the notice boards to get a feel for the culture of the organisation. Visiting one office recently I was intrigued to see that 'Staff Assertiveness Training' was being programmed for one of the lunch hours that week. I hadn't encountered that before and my first reaction was to laugh. Did we really need *training* on how to be assertive? That morning I had been playing with my grand-daughter, who had worked out very early how to assert herself, at the age of two!

I asked why such 'assertiveness training' was needed. It turned out that there were a number of people in the organisation who felt marginalised, minorities by gender, race or culture, whose voices were not getting properly heard. They needed coaching on how to communicate their views firmly but without giving unnecessary offence ... fair enough!

But that set me thinking: how assertive should the Christian be at work? What place is there at work for the sort of humility that the New Testament encourages, particularly when you find yourself working for a difficult boss? Alexander Hill asks: 'Is there a place for humble people in the corporate world today? Or are they victims in waiting, the next roadkill on the capitalist highway?'[1]

How do we deal with those in authority over us?

Meekness

'All of you, clothe yourselves with humility toward one another because, "God opposes the proud but shows favour to the humble". Humble yourselves therefore under God's mighty hand, that he may lift you up in due time' (1 Pet. 5:5-6).

That seems clear enough! But how do we apply biblical teaching about submission and humility to the rough and tumble of work? Do we just ignore it; or dilute it? How do we take it seriously? My experience tells me that in negotiating contracts with construction contractors, or between employers and labour unions, we don't typically see a lot of submission or humility in action from either side!

Jesus said: *'Blessed are the meek for they will inherit the earth'* (Matt. 5:5). But how do we exercise meekness? It is a word easy to misunderstand. It is NOT weakness. I like the description the late John Stott gave in speaking about Jesus' words in the Sermon on the Mount ... 'Meekness': he said, 'is the gentleness of the truly strong'. I take it to mean operating with respect and courtesy, seeking peaceful solutions wherever possible, not paying back wrong for wrong, not trading insults. If you like sporting analogies; it means 'playing the ball and not the player'.

---

1. Alexander Hill, *Just Business* (IVP, 2009), p. 30.

It's interesting to see how the Apostle Paul interpreted Jesus' teaching about meekness and submission. Certainly, he did not lie down like a doormat for others to walk on. In several situations he asserted his legal rights as a Roman citizen and as a member of the public under law. There was the time when he claimed his rights as a Roman citizen to prevent an unjust flogging (Acts 22:25). On another occasion in Philippi, when those citizenship rights had been ignored, he demanded the city leaders come and apologise to him after they had realised their mistake and were now trying to cover it up. They offered to smuggle him out of the city by the back door. Paul replied:

> 'They beat us publicly without a trial, even though we are Roman citizens, and threw us into prison. And now do they want to get rid of us quietly? No! Let them come themselves and escort us out' (Acts 16:37).

Remember also how, in theological debate, Paul publicly opposed the Apostle Peter when he thought he was wrong (Gal. 2:14). He didn't back away from expressing his views, even though it led to sharp disagreement (Acts 15:2).

When to assert? When to submit? We all need God's wisdom in such testing situations. As always, Jesus points us in the right direction. He said, 'So in everything, do to others what you would have them do to you, for this sums up the Law and the Prophets' (Matt. 7:12).

Think what this means in your workplace in practice. Do you like those who work for you to: undermine your authority at every opportunity; snipe at you behind your back; not give you the support you need? Presumably not! Then why treat your boss like that?

Rather, do you like those who work for *you* to: support you; do their task reliably and responsibly; have the courage to tell you when you are wrong; work as a team member rather than in isolation? Then why not treat your boss like that?

Questions

1. What has been the biggest challenge in your work experience of submitting to authority? What did you learn from it? How did you handle it? How as a Christian might you have handled it better?

2. In what situations have you had to 'stand your ground' and assert your rights, or stand up for the rights of others?

3. In what situations have you had to learn to submit to authority?

19. Bullying and Harassment

'There is a cowardly propensity in the human heart that delights in oppressing someone else, and in the gratification of this base desire we always select a victim that can be outraged with safety.'[2]

These words were spoken by James T. Rapier, a congressman from Alabama, in a speech arguing for passage of the Civil Rights Bill in the USA in 1874. They go right to the heart of the cause of so much bullying in so many situations.

When I lived in the East African bush, I would sometimes see a pack of wild dogs chasing a herd of impala. They had a clear and ruthless strategy. They would instinctively and collectively fix on one animal in the herd that they were chasing, usually the weakest. They would not normally change targets mid-chase. As a pack, they would go after their selected target and kill it. In some ways it's a picture of typical group bullying: pick on the weakest or the one isolated from the rest. At least the wild dogs were doing it because they needed the food. When human beings act like that, they have no such excuses. It's just a very ugly manifestation of human sinfulness.

'Government minister stood aside for bullying… accusation levied by his chief of staff.' That's the headline of today's newspaper as I write this. The same paper carries a story about a leading surgeon, similarly accused. Last week there was a story about yet another attempt to stamp out bullying of young recruits in the military. If I switch channels on TV, I see more stories of sexual harassment and assault of women by males in power positions and abuse of vulnerable children. Human weakness and propensity to bully and harass others are on public display on a regular basis.

---

2. Cited in J. Daley, *Great speeches by African Americans*' (Dover Publications, 2006), p. 61.

Bullying happens wherever groups of people gather. We usually encounter it first in our schooldays. It takes different forms; intimidation, physical or mental cruelty, or 'initiation ceremonies'. Many who have survived education in single-sex boarding schools have experienced bullying as an accepted norm. Many more have been bullied at school because of their race, their disability, their sexual orientation or just for the way they look, or dress. The twelve-year-old daughter of a friend of ours was being encouraged by her mother to make some new friends. The girl had seen the destructive effects of group bullying on her older sister and told her mother, 'I don't want friends. They are all mean and horrible. I'll just get bullied'. Bullying damages young lives. Such experiences are not quickly forgotten.

Bullying in the workplace is experienced in a variety of ways. It may be verbal abuse, being shouted down in a conversation; being labelled in a derogatory way 'O you're just a xxxx!' It might include belittling of your beliefs and ideas, ridicule of the way you dress or your physical appearance. You may be intentionally humiliated in front of others or have your contribution persistently criticised and undervalued. Or maybe you just don't fit in because you refuse to follow the group's agenda. It may take the form of 'cyber bullying', getting 'trolled' on social media. Bullying may also include physical violence, or at least aggressive body language, to intimidate you with the threat of violence. It may be by an individual, or by a group working together like a pack of wild dogs, to isolate and hurt a single individual.

Even Jesus experienced bullying. He knows what it feels like. It was part of the suffering He willingly endured in taking on our humanness and in laying down His life to save sinners: *'the men who were guarding Jesus began mocking and beating him. They blindfolded him and demanded, "Prophesy! Who hit you?" And they said many other insulting things to him'* (Luke 22:63-65).

Human nature has not changed over the past 2,000 years. Survivors of prison camps and interrogation in secret police cells testify to similar experiences today, even in countries with a supposed Christian culture. It's a familiar story of abuse of power, ganging up

on vulnerable individuals, using them as a source of cruel 'fun'; a mix of mockery, verbal and physical abuse. The common theme is a lack of moral accountability of the bullies. The soldiers bullying Jesus knew they could get away with it. This is one reason why it is so hard to stamp out bullying in workplaces. Whatever processes are introduced, the victims are often unwilling to confront the perpetrators or to register a formal complaint, in case it makes their situation worse. They fear that they will be made to feel even more isolated and vulnerable. The bullies then get away with it.

Dealing with bullies

Most good workplaces these days have policies to prevent bullying and procedures to deal with it. This typically involves a stepped process, requiring the victim or workmate to report the matter to a supervisor, directly or via a complaints hotline. This may then lead to counselling for both parties and disciplinary action for the bully. The best processes involve some form of restoration of the relationship between the bully and the victim. If you are being bullied, you may need to get help from a professional counsellor. If it has reached a level of criminality, then you will need to go to the police. There is no shortage of good advice and wise counsel out there. But what does the gospel say to us at this point that is distinctively Christian?

Firstly, we can talk to God about it in prayer: *'Cast all your anxiety on him because he cares for you'* (1 Pet. 5:7).

Secondly, we are to pray for the bully. Jesus said: *'You have heard that it was said, "Love your neighbor and hate your enemy". But I tell you, love your enemies and pray for those who persecute you'* (Matt. 5:43, 44).

We may also need to pray for wisdom in our own responses and, like the psalmist, ask God to intervene in the situation on our behalf: *'Defend the weak and the fatherless: uphold the cause of the poor and the oppressed'* (Ps. 82:3).

It's also a good idea to share the problem, and your hurt, with someone you love and trust. We are to *'carry each other's burdens, and in this way you will fulfill the law of Christ'* (Gal. 6:2). This is one of the blessings of friendship, and of Christian fellowship in particular.

Finally, we are to act. Don't let hurt and bitterness fester inside you. Don't give the devil a foothold through your bad experience. Your self-esteem may take a battering initially, but remind yourself each day that you are made in the image of God. You are loved by Him.

Bullying and harassment can leave scars that take a long time to heal. But we have the promise of God that He will bring us through. These words were written to Christians who were being bullied and persecuted, *'And the God of all grace, who called you to his eternal glory in Christ, after you have suffered a little while, will himself restore you and make you strong, firm and steadfast'* (1 Pet. 5:10).

Self-check: am I a bully?

It's one thing to get angry and aggressive when we see bullies playing power games with other people's lives. But, as we do, we might ask ourselves … 'Am I a bully?' Bullying can sometimes be unconscious. It's not always a matter of evil intent. If we have any power over another human being, then we need to be very careful how we use it.

- If you are physically large or strong, then be aware of the effect your presence may have on smaller or weaker people;

- If you are intellectually smart, then be aware of the way you deal with those less able to grasp the point, or see the issues as quickly and clearly as you see them, especially in open meetings;

- If you are sure you are right, then be wise in the way you treat those with different opinions. No one likes being shouted down or made to feel a fool, especially in front of others;

- If you have 'a way with words' then be aware of the power of your words to inflict harm, intentionally, and in thoughtless asides;

- If you are well accepted in your group of colleagues and friends, then be sensitive to those who are outside your inner circle. Make a point of including them rather than ignoring them.

- In all we do, we need to be thoughtful and respectful in the way we treat people in the workplace.

Let's guard ourselves against bullying and harassing others, consciously or unconsciously, and pray for wisdom and courage to deal with bullies at work.

Questions

1. What experiences of bullying or harassment have you had in your life, or seen at your workplace?

2. How have these been dealt with?

3. How can you act to help prevent bullying in your situation?

20. Dealing with Conflict

'Blessed are the peacemakers for they will be called children of God' (Matt. 5:9).

Whenever two people strongly assert opposing views there is conflict. When personalities clash, there is conflict. In most workplaces, including the home, there is conflict. How do you handle it? That's a commonly asked 'test question' at job interviews. How do you deal with angry customers, difficult parents, impossible bosses?

Flee, fight or fudge are the classic responses. Do you back down and run away? Do you enter the debate aggressively or, do you avoid the issues and just try to suppress all the resentment simmering away inside? How do you respond to someone who is deliberately confrontational, who puts you on to the back foot and makes you feel like you have to apologise just for holding a contrary opinion?

For those of us who like to get stuck into an argument, let's remember we may score some easy points, but at what cost? We might win a battle, but 'lose the war' by damaging a relationship irreparably. Sometimes, it's not what we say that creates strife, it's the way we say it. The book of Proverbs wisely observes *'A gentle answer turns away wrath but a harsh word stirs up anger'* (15:1). The way we respond to intentionally provocative behaviour either calms or inflames the situation.

Bottling it up, leaving a lot of issues unresolved, is not usually a good route. It's sad to see people seething with discontent, eaten up with bitterness about the way they've been treated and quietly pursuing an agenda to get their revenge.

What about resolving conflict between others? For parents and teachers, stopping war breaking out in the classroom, or in the playroom at home, is a daily test of wisdom and patience. What happens when you have a good relationship with two people at work … A and B? Say A

and B are in conflict and both want you to take their side. What do you do? Do you succumb to the pressure to compromise one relationship, just to make the other person feel better?

Conflict may be part of your job. If you are in the armed forces or the police, it is likely to involve physical conflict. If you are a politician, lawyer or social worker, or if your job involves difficult negotiations with unions or management groups over workers' rights, the nature of the conflict will be more mental and emotional. Sometimes conflict is unavoidable, but it is often emotionally and physically draining.

Necessary conflict

Sometimes, conflict is necessary and constructive. We may need to actually provoke conflict by taking a stand against something that is plainly unjust, or confronting someone with their wrong-doing. This was the approach of the Old Testament prophets who spoke out boldly against injustice. For them it was not 'peace at any price'.

For example when the prophet Amos verbally attacked the wealthy women of his day: *'Hear this you cows of Bashan ... you women who oppress the poor and crush the needy'* (Amos 4:1), he was clearly more concerned about God's justice than good public relations!

John the Baptist followed in that same prophetic tradition. When he saw the crowds coming out to the desert to be baptised, his opening remarks were hardly welcoming: *'You brood of vipers, who warned you to flee from the coming wrath?'* (Luke 3:7). He warned them about trusting in their religious traditions, rather than living out their faith with integrity (3:8) and he called them to change. His boldness eventually cost him his life.

Jesus Himself often confronted the religious leaders publicly, *'Woe to you teachers of the law ..., you hypocrites! You shut the door of the kingdom of heaven in people's faces'* (Matt. 23:13).

Paul did not shy away from conflict when he made a public stand in the Council of Jerusalem for the truth of the gospel against those who wanted to enforce religious legalism on new Christians (Acts 15). That situation shows us that truth and wisdom can emerge from conflict situations which involve robust discussion.

In the history of the church over the past 2,000 years, many have suffered and died in conflict with the state or religious authorities, just for standing up for what they believed.

Sometimes conflict is necessary ....

Unnecessary conflict

... But, much conflict is unhelpful and unnecessary.

When we are tired, or just having a bad day, we might be tempted to get drawn into petty arguments about coffee cups, parking spaces, or workmates not doing their fair share. Isn't it the case that little things often cause more arguments than seemingly more important issues? Our human self-centredness inevitably creates a lot of strife. '*What causes fights and quarrels among you? Don't they come from your desires that battle within you?*' (James 4:1). Given that we naturally want to get our own way, it's easy to stir up jealousy by casual dismissive remarks; or besmirch people's character with innuendo, or enlarge the faults of others while ignoring or minimising our own.

The manager of a construction company was bemoaning the unnecessarily confrontational nature of the industry he was in, and the negative effect it was having on his staff. He said to me, 'Our people don't want to have to come to work every day just to fight. There is a better way.'

The book of Proverbs tells us a lot about dealing with conflict, particularly in terms of what we say and how we say it: '*The words of the reckless pierce like swords, but the tongue of the wise brings healing*' (12:18).

Proverbs also warns us about the danger of gossip in ruining friendships and creating unnecessary conflict: '*A perverse person stirs up dissension and a gossip separates close friends*' *(16:28)*. It reminds us that unwise words add fuel to the fire of strife and discontent: '*As charcoal to embers and as wood to fire, so is a quarrelsome person for kindling strife*' (26:21).

Sometimes holding our tongue and keeping silent is the wisest response: '*Sin is not ended by multiplying words, but the prudent hold their tongues*' (10:19). Sometimes, in conflict situations, 'silence is golden'.

Knowing when conflict is unavoidable; understanding what issues are worth fighting for and which ones are just 'sweating the small stuff'; knowing when, what, and how to speak in these situations, all test our energy, our relationships and our wisdom.

When we are tired and stressed after a long day, it's more likely that we will say things we regret and lash out at people unfairly. These words from James in the New Testament have a practical application in most workplaces on most days:

> '... where you have envy and selfish ambition, there you find disorder and every evil practice. But the wisdom that comes from heaven is first of all pure, then peace-loving, considerate, submissive, full of mercy and good fruit, impartial and sincere. Peace makers who sow in peace reap a harvest of righteousness' (James 3:16-18).

Questions

1. In your experience, what positive things have come out of conflict situations at work?

2. In what situations have you been drawn into conflict which ended badly? How might you have dealt with those situations more wisely?

3. In what situations have you seen others exercise a God-given wisdom in resolving conflict? What have you learned from those experiences?

21. The Blame Game

'But the people were thirsty for water and they grumbled against Moses. They said, "Why did you bring us up out of Egypt to make us and our children and livestock die of thirst?"' (Exod. 17:3).

Whose fault is it?

If you have been in the workforce for any length of time, or been part of a social club, community group or even a Christian church, you will have encountered the blame game. When we are under pressure and things go wrong, we naturally look for someone to blame. How people position themselves in these games, which are played out every day in almost every workplace (and in many homes!) reveals a lot about character. When there is a problem and the boss asks; 'who is responsible? Who failed to do their job? Who made the error?' Do you duck for cover and point the finger at someone else or take responsibility when you know you are at fault?

You might know this classic summary of the six stages of a typical project:

1. Enthusiasm
2. Disillusionment
3. Panic
4. Search for the guilty
5. Punishment of the innocent
6. Praise and honour for the non-participants

Cynical? Yes ... but often true. Playing the blame game is the opposite of being accountable (see Chap. 10). It destroys unity and wrecks relationships.

Fear of failure, or admission of failure, is ingrained in some work cultures. It stifles initiative and creativity because nobody wants to be

seen to fail. It makes for tense, stagnant, unhappy workplaces. In an attempt to overcome this negativity, some organisations try to develop a 'no blame' culture, to encourage people to own up to their mistakes and feel confident that they won't be victimised by failure if they have given their best.

The success of these initiatives depends on how they are followed through. When people make mistakes, are they assured that 'the one who never made a mistake never made anything' and encouraged to press on, or are they publicly humiliated? 'No blame' cultures are stress-tested when the first crisis comes along. Human nature being what it is, we may quickly revert to type and scatter blame in all directions!

Human nature

According to the Bible, the blame game started right back in the Garden of Eden. When God asked Adam and Eve why they had eaten the for-bidden fruit, the one and only thing that God had told them not to do, the man replied, *'The woman you put here with me—she gave me some fruit from the tree and I ate it'* (Gen. 3:12). Then the woman said, *'The serpent deceived me, and I ate'* (v. 13). So Adam blames Eve, and indirectly blames God also, and Eve blames the serpent who tempted her.

The Genesis story gives us great insight into human nature. When things go wrong, the desire to exonerate ourselves from responsibility and blame the other guy is deeply ingrained in all of us. Playing the blame game comes quite naturally.

Admitting to fault or failure of any sort is seen by some as admission of weakness. Some trainers in negotiating techniques counsel us to NEVER admit that we are wrong or to blame. It weakens our negotiating position they say. But for the Christian, to accept blame when it is our fault is part of living with honesty and with integrity.

Hindsight is a wonderful thing. When things go 'pear-shaped', the lawsuits and public enquiries which typically follow can turn quickly from the pursuit of justice into a witch hunt. It's very stress-ful and often grossly unfair, when people who are in the front line, making hard decisions in good faith, are then heavily criticised by those who have never themselves been put in such stressful decision-making situations.

The cover up

A close friend of the 'blame game' is the 'cover up'. You might think we human beings would learn that trying to cover up mistakes, or deliberate wrongdoing, usually leads to much greater trouble than the original problem being covered up. But the same mistakes keep recurring. The Watergate scandal, and all the '…. gate' scandals which have followed, which hit our TV screens and media feeds are a regular reminder.

In the infrastructure business I worked in, we learned that clients could accept that we might make mistakes so long as we owned up as quickly as possible and committed to putting it right at our expense. This is where simple honesty and good business happily coexist. What clients could not forgive, and what they certainly never forgot, was when someone tried to cover up and, delay, or try to avoid, telling the client the bad news. I shall never forget sitting in a meeting with about thirty people on a major oil project when one of the engineering firms involved in the project made the mistake of sending in a junior manager to convey the bad news that the access road to the plant was going to cost four times the original estimate. The silence which followed that announcement was deafening! Everyone was looking at the floor or studying their papers intently, waiting for the oil boss to erupt in anger—which he duly did! The firm concerned made three big mistakes. First, they chose the wrong setting to break the bad news, second the senior person responsible did not attend the meeting, instead leaving a junior to take the inevitable criticism. Third, they blamed the problem on another company which had provided the original estimate. In football terms, it was like kicking three own goals! One doesn't forget life lessons like that!

Bringing mistakes out into the open, taking responsibility and committing to fix problems is an expression of simple integrity in any workplace. Blaming someone else and covering up mistakes may be our default, 'knee jerk' reaction. It may 'seem like a good idea at the time'—but it never is.

The rarely read, and quite difficult, book of Numbers in the Old Testament contains this very simple statement which surely has timeless application:

'… *be sure that your sin will find you out*' (Num. 32:23).

Setting an example

Bad leaders blame others, so do bad team members. If you have played any team sport, you know that when players start blaming each other for mistakes, the game is lost.

By contrast, a leader worth following is down in the trenches with you when the going is tough, not up in their office on the fifty-second floor writing emails to their boss to protect themselves.

The most valuable team members at work are not always the most gifted. The ones who will take responsibility, shun the blame game, and quietly set about fixing the problem, are like gold.

Questions

1. When have you seen the 'blame game' played out at your workplace?

2. In what situations is your default position to start to blame others?

3. Have you ever been blamed for something that was not your fault? How did you react?

4. How do the principles of accountability we looked at in chapter 9 help us avoid playing 'the blame game'?

22. Exploitation

'A ruler who oppresses the poor is like a driving rain that leaves no crops' (Prov. 28:3).

Abuse of power

At one level exploitation in the workplace is just a form of economic bullying. It's abuse of power 'because I can'.

Unregulated, unfettered business will usually lead to exploitation because that's the way greedy human nature will take it. As Ryken comments, 'When work is viewed as an economic commodity that is bought and sold, exploitation is a natural result unless other factors are strong enough to counter it'.[3]

The (generally) higher cost of labour in developed countries leads multinationals to outsource and move labour-intensive production to lower cost countries. If human labour can be bought for a lower price in one part of the world, then, naturally, companies will take advantage of that in the best interest of their shareholders.

There is of course a much darker side to exploitation, the abuse and trafficking of young women and children in the sex trade, and the widespread practice of slavery generally. The United Nations reported[4] that there were 40 million people in slavery and 152 million children in forced child labour in 2017.

Do we criticise exploitation, but remain blind to how much we benefit from it? We might be surprised and self-righteous when such exploitation is exposed in a TV documentary about sweat factories paying their employees a pittance to produce shoes, or coffee plantations paying exploitative wages to pickers working long

---

3. Leland Ryken, *Work and Leisure in Christian Perspective*, (Wipf and Stock Publishers, 2002), p. 72.

4. 'Global Estimates of Modern Slavery'. ILO, 2017.

hours—but we don't complain too loudly because we like the shoes and enjoy the coffee.

Closer to home

It's easy to condemn exploitation elsewhere. It's sometimes harder to recognise, or admit to, closer to home. There are some obvious signs to look out for:

- workers not getting paid, fairly, in full and on time: all too common for casual workers with limited recourse
- being forced to work longer hours with no regard to the worker's health or family situation
- having to do someone else's job as well as your own for no extra pay
- being instructed to 'turn a blind eye' to workplace health and safety laws to save cost
- being 'encouraged' to provide sexual favours in exchange for keeping your job

You don't have to look further than your daily newsfeed to find examples of each of these forms of exploitation.

Making a difference

What difference can a Christian make here? It may seem like trying to stem a raging river with a few bags of sand, but we need to make our stand somewhere, both at the personal level and in changing the culture of our workplace, so far as we can.

Some get actively involved in politics, directly or through pressure groups. Christians continue to be at the forefront of relief agencies caring for vulnerable women and children and in setting up self-supporting businesses to provide income in poor areas. Journalists also play an important role in exposing exploitation to a wider audience through the media.

In our own workplace, we can blow the whistle on exploitation and take a stand with those being unjustly treated.

At the consumer end of the chain, organisations like Fairtrade, which work to 'secure a better deal for farmers and workers', market

products which they can certify as coming from countries and businesses where workers are paid a living wage. It's certainly a start.

Exploitation of the poor

Back in the nineteenth century, Engels highlighted a different type of slavery in which workers are trapped in a situation of being alienated from the results of their work, *'Nothing is more terrible than being constrained to do some one thing every day from morning until night against one's will .... Why does he work? For love of work? From a natural impulse? Not at all! He works for money, for a thing which has nothing whatsoever to do with the work itself'.*[5]

We can just shrug off that form of alienation which Engels describes, as 'just the way it is', 'the result of market forces' or 'good business'. But the Bible makes clear that God hates exploitation of the poor. He warns those creating working conditions which reduce the dignity of people made in the image of God that they will have to account to Him for their actions. God cares about widows, children and orphans. He hates injustice. God expressed His anger against exploitation through His prophet Amos in these words, which need no explanation:

> *'They sell the innocent for silver, and the needy for a pair of sandals. They trample on the heads of the poor as on the dust of the ground and deny justice to the oppressed'* (Amos 2:6-7).

The book of Proverbs highlights care for the poor as a hallmark of righteousness ... i.e., of being in right relationship with God: *'The righteous care about justice for the poor, but the wicked have no such concern'* (Prov. 29:7). Exploitation of the poor and disadvantaged is explicitly condemned, *'Do not exploit the poor because they are poor and do not crush the needy in court'* (22:22) ... and *'A ruler who oppresses the poor is like a driving rain that leaves no crops'* (28:3).

The responsibility of anyone entrusted with decision-making authority which affects the lives of others, is clear. We are not to misuse the power granted to us to oppress or take advantage of others.

---

5. F. Engels, *The Condition of the Working Class in England in 1844*, (Sonnenschein & Co, 1892), p. 118.

We are accountable to God for the way we treat people. If we are an employer, we are to pay fair wages, on time and in full.

Role models

Nehemiah, the Old Testament leader called by God to rebuild the walls of Jerusalem, and then to govern the city, is a particular hero of mine. He stands as a great role model of a leader who refused to use his position of power for his own gain, despite a clear precedent from earlier exploitative leaders. He wrote this:

> *'But the earlier governors—those preceding me—placed a heavy burden on the people and took forty shekels of silver from them in addition to food and wine. Their assistants also lorded it over the people. But out of reverence for God I did not act like that'* (Neh. 5:15).

Let's note Nehemiah's twofold motivation for making this stand. He refused to place a heavy burden on the people who were already 'doing it tough' (5:19). But underlying that action was his deep sense of accountability to God. *'Out of reverence for God, I did not act like that.'* His faith made a difference to the way he did his job and the way he treated those under him. In making that stand he was honouring God publicly. He knew that his role as leader was to serve the people for their good, not to exploit them.

But, we don't have to look back in the pages of history to find examples of leaders and organisations who value their employees and treat them well and who use their power as those accountable to God. Thank God ... there are many present day 'Nehemiahs'.

Questions

1. Take a check on the way you exercise any position of authority you hold (at work, in the community or in the home). Are there ways in which you abuse that power?

2. If someone knew nothing about your professed faith, what would they learn about you from the way you treat people?

3. In what ways can we act and change our behaviour to reduce exploitation?

23. Loneliness

'Never will I leave you; never will I forsake you' (Heb. 13:5).

A growing problem

In April 2018, the UK Government appointed the world's first Minister for Loneliness. It was an initiative which recognised the growing problem of this twenty-first-century disease. In announcing the appointment, the British Prime Minister commented, *'For far too many people, loneliness is the sad reality of modern life'*.

In the USA, a report by CIGNA concluded that 'America's loneliness epidemic is getting worse'.[6] It identified the causes of loneliness at work as 'lack of social support, too few meaningful interactions, poor physical and mental health and a lack of balance in our lives'. No real surprises there. Other countries, including Japan, and Australia, are increasingly concerned about loneliness as a public health concern. One leading social researcher identified the growing link between loneliness and anxiety.[7] Increasing workforce mobility is adding to the problem for the obvious reason that changing jobs frequently makes it harder to build friendships with workmates. Writing this in yet another Covid lockdown, I wonder what the long-term effects will be on families, workplaces and communities of so much enforced isolation.

But let me just focus here on the experience of being lonely at work. If you are a single parent whose work is raising children and looking after the home, you may feel you are missing out badly on social interaction with other adults. If you are one of the army of freelancers, working alone at home you might enjoy the freedom of managing

---

6. 'Loneliness and its impact on the American Workplace' CIGNA, March 2020.

7. Hugh Mackay, *Australia Reimagined—towards a more compassionate less anxious society* (Macmillan, 2018).

your own time but at the same time feel isolated and miss the 'buzz' of working with others in a group.

But loneliness is not necessarily the same as 'being by yourself'. In my early twenties, I worked for two years in a Game Reserve in Tanzania. My home was a one-man tent in the African bush, but I don't recall ever feeling lonely. I suspect loneliness is more about a lack of meaningful relationships and the feeling of being cut-off and excluded. You might work for a large organisation and still be lonely. You can be surrounded by people all day but unable to share problems with anyone in any depth. You may have a strong marriage and family life and still feel lonely at work because you don't want to unload all your work problems on your family when you get home, but you have no one else to share them with.

Even if you belong to a great church you may have no one to 'open up' to. It's not always easy to find people or situations where you are comfortable sharing some of the complex ethical, technical and people problems you have to deal with that are so draining. Are they interested enough to listen? Are they able to understand? You may be the custodian of confidential information which can't be shared so you can't talk about those issues anyway. On Sundays, you greet someone at church and they ask how you are going. 'Fine, thanks', you say, because you don't think they would readily appreciate what you are going through at work. So you lie awake at night worrying and not coming up with the answers.

In those sorts of situations loneliness is not necessarily immediately obvious. Scratch the surface of those who present an image of happy fulfilment at work, at church or on social media. You might find that underneath that veneer, their life is falling apart, and they badly need support and friendship.

One of the best support groups I have encountered was at our church in Dubai. A group of us met for breakfast, every Saturday morning. We were all away from our homeland. Many were away from family and marriage partners back home. Most were grappling with very difficult work issues. We shared problems and we prayed about them. One morning, a man whose small business was failing, broke down in tears. After composing himself he returned, looked around

the room and simply said, 'This group is a place of integrity'. He knew he was no longer facing his problems alone.

Friendship and 'fellowship'

The Bible has wonderful, game-changing good news for us.

Firstly, we have the promise of Jesus that He will always be with us. As we read the gospels, we find that Jesus experienced so many of the human problems we face. In His awful suffering and death, He was completely alone. One of His friends betrayed Him, one denied Him and the rest ran away. On the cross He cried out in utter desolation *'My God My God why have you forsaken me?'* (Matt. 27:46). Whatever we have to go through in life, we will never be as totally alone as Jesus. He left us with the *promise 'I am with you always to the very end of the age'* (28:20).

Secondly, there is God's gift of friendship, part of His common grace to all His creatures. Caring friendships enrich our lives and affirm our humanity. We need each other. Committed friendships at their best, when we are there for each other no matter what, reflect Jesus' promise of friendship with us. We might feel like sinking into the mire of self-pity, 'no one phones me up, no one is interested in my life', but maybe we need to take a practical step, make the first move and risk rejection. Isn't there one person at our workplace that we can befriend, someone we can meet for a coffee or take for a drink after work? Is there someone outside our work environment that we can share with and trust?

Thirdly, there is Christian fellowship. Tolkien famously wrote about 'The Fellowship of the Ring', a small group of people committed to a high-risk mission. The Bible speaks about the 'Fellowship of the Holy Spirit' (2 Cor. 13:14), a large group of people bonded together by a common faith in Jesus Christ. It's a bond which transcends age, gender, and racial and cultural boundaries.

When I became a Christian, I found a whole new horizon of relationships opened up. I started to realise that though Christian faith is personal, it is not private. If I belong to Christ, I also belong to His people. The Bible never expresses this in terms of membership of an institution, but rather belonging to a global family, a fellowship

of believers, drawn from *every nation, tribe, people and language*' (Rev. 7:9). I have lived and worked for extended periods in several different countries. Wherever I go, I find a common bond with Christians, whatever their age, colour, culture or nationality.

Belonging to God's people is one of the great blessings of Christian faith. But ... while we enjoy this friendship and fellowship for ourselves, we have a responsibility to reach out to lonely people. I have been reading John's gospel recently and reminded again how much time and energy Jesus spent with individuals: Nicodemus (Chap. 3), the Samaritan woman (Chap. 4), the disabled man (Chap. 5), the man born blind (Chap. 9), Peter on the seashore (Chap. 21). So much of the gospel is taken up with these in-depth, one-to-one conversations. Isn't this a great encouragement to all of us to invest our time in one-to-one friendships?

In the gospels we also see Jesus making time for people isolated and excluded from society—lonely people. There was the woman with an incurable haemorrhage who had spent all her money on doctors. At the other end of the social spectrum was a wealthy, but seemingly friendless, tax collector. Most striking of all is the way Jesus reached out to the lepers of His day, those excluded and cut off from family and work and with no hope for the future.

Whatever our situation, there will always be opportunities to demonstrate to lonely and isolated people the quality of friendship, unconditional love and care that God gives to us.

Questions

1. Is there someone you can meet with regularly for coffee or a meal to share the issues you are facing at work, to pray and encourage one another?

2. Is there a group you can join (or start) for the purpose of prayer and mutual support?

3. Is there a lonely person at your workplace that you can reach out to?

PART D
TESTING SITUATIONS

PART D
TESTING STUDENTS

> *'I started to see my work more as a crucible where God was pounding and grinding and refining, rather than as a place where I was actively and effectively serving him.'*[1]

Sometimes work can be especially tough. We get stressed by the impossible demands placed on us, frustrated by the customers, the bureaucracy or the abusive students, or bored with the repetitive nature of our task. We feel trapped at home, or in a job from which we can't escape. We can't afford to leave and we're not sure we can get another job easily. Or, we may feel pressured to conform to the culture of our organisation, to the extent that we compromise our beliefs, and our behaviour.

As we reflect on our experience of work, it may look like there are more low points than high points, with no way forward and no way out. We start to see ourselves as failures in our career and our witness. We hit rock bottom when we are made 'redundant'.

Does that all sound depressing? Well, thank God He has something to say to us, to teach us in every situation. He has promised to never leave us to battle on alone, and He has promised that His grace is sufficient for every need.

More than that, His purpose in our lives is to produce gold.

The words of many popular worship songs (old and new) are prayers to God, asking Him to 'purify our heart', 'change us', to 'mould us' like a potter moulds the clay. They express the Bible's teaching that the Holy Spirit of God is at work in our lives, not just in church, not just in spiritual moments of prayer and worship, but in the daily stress and challenge of life—including work—to make us more like Jesus.

---

1. Katherine Leary Alsdorf in Foreword to T. Keller *Every Good Endeavour'*, p. 13.

Way back in the fifth century Augustine wrote, '... *when He exposes us to adversities, it is either to prove our perfections or correct our imperfections...*'.[2] I have often thought how good it would be if God would simply change me in a 'one off' special experience and avoid all those difficulties of 'proving' and 'correction'. But of course life isn't like that, and God doesn't promise that. He *has* promised to change us progressively into His likeness (2 Cor. 3:18) and one of the ways He does that is through testing experiences at work.

2. Augustine of Hippo, ed. Marcus Dods *Works, The City of God, Volume I* (Hamilton, Adams and Co.: London) I, p. 29.

24. Trapped

'Remember my chains ...' (Col. 4:18).

It's an awful feeling being trapped, being locked into a situation from which you see no escape.

Perhaps at this point you might wonder what I am taking about. If you don't like the job, why not just resign and walk out? But those who feel trapped know all too well what I mean. You may have few marketable skills or qualifications, limited mobility or lack of opportunity. You may be loaded with debt and tied to a job you hate, terrified of being fired because unemployment in your town is running at 25 per cent. You may be in debt, caught in a poverty trap and have to keep working to pay the rent. One or more of these real-life situations might sound familiar:

- The security worker at the airport: she has no skills, training or qualifications. She is a single parent with two children. She is focused on keeping her job in the face of recent cut-backs and on feeding her kids and keeping them at school. She dreams of one day moving to a safer area with fewer drug problems.

- The farmer facing a third successive year of drought ... massively in debt to his bankers. He can't sell the farm and he lies awake at night worrying how to repay the loan.

- The parent or carer with 24/7 responsibility for a disabled member of the family. A friend who is in this situation shared in one particularly low moment, 'I feel trapped in a tunnel with no escape until I die'.

- The mid-level manager, with a mortgage, car loan, and a maxed-out credit card. She is stressed out and hates her job but isn't confident she can find another.

- The expatriate nanny/housemaid working in a country with no labour laws and few human rights. Her passport is 'held' by the host family as a condition of her employment.

- People with disabilities who have difficulty finding *any* job at all.

- 'Sweat factories' in so many countries, where people work long hours for survival wages.

- Fly-in-fly-out workers on remote mining projects. They have a big mortgage and need the work. They worry about the effect on their marriages of having to spend weeks, and sometimes months, away from family.

If you are not aware of any of these experiences of being trapped in a job and longing to escape, then you must lead a very sheltered life. You need to get out more!

Freedom

What has the gospel to say to us here? We are used to reading the New Testament on our smart phones or tablets, or in our nice leather-bound Bibles, but the harsh reality is that much of it is in the form of letters, written from prison, to churches which included slaves. Paul encouraged them, *'If you can gain your freedom, do so'* (1 Cor. 7:21).

But what if we can't get free from our particular situation? Paul himself spent long years in prison for his faith. In one of his prison letters, he asked the Christians at Colossae to *'remember my chains'* (Col. 4:18). He must have longed to get out, but he wrote these magnificent words, *'I have learned to be content whatever the circumstances. I know what it is to be in need, and I know what it is to have plenty. I have learned the secret of being content in any and every situation, whether well-fed or hungry, whether living in plenty or in want. I can do all this through him who gives me strength'* (Phil. 4:11-13).

Where did he learn to cope with such difficult situations? Not at school, or in a lifestyle seminar. He learned it with the help of God through hard, testing experiences of deprivation and imprisonment.

With our natural love of comfort and pleasure, this is a reality we don't like facing up to.

Our experience of feeling trapped in a work situation, however bad, can't readily be compared with the awful experience of being in prison, but we can learn from Paul's attitude. He encourages believers that '*it is for freedom that Christ has set us free*' (Gal. 5:1) and reminds us that '*where the Spirit of the Lord is, there is freedom ...*' (2 Cor. 3:17).

Paul discovered a different type of freedom: freedom from fear, from condemnation, from religious legalism. This is a freedom of the spirit, which only God can give and which no one can take from us.

When Professor F. F. Bruce, the English Bible scholar, wrote his 'opus magnus' on the ministry and message of the Apostle Paul, he called it 'The Apostle of the Heart Set Free'.[3] I love that title, because Paul didn't just talk about it and write about it, he lived it.

What are the options?

If you feel trapped in a dead-end position at work, or trapped in a care role at home, what choices are open to you?

Firstly, *you can stay as you are,* where you are, sink deeper into your rut and just grumble and complain to anyone who will listen at how bad life is treating you.

Or, *God may want you to do something else or move somewhere else.* When you are looking for a new job, the grass usually looks greener over the other side of the fence—at least at first. But, moving isn't necessarily the right answer. We can change jobs, move cities or countries, and simply take our problems with us.

We may take for granted the opportunity to move between jobs, but this isn't so in many cultures, especially for those with low levels of education and limited access to interesting opportunities.

The third possibility is that *God wants you to stay right where you are and change your whole attitude.* Maybe God wants a new person in your job and that person is YOU. Perhaps, He wants you to start to do your work 'for the Lord' and 'in His Name' and to see your workplace as where God wants you to be right now.

---

3. Published by William B. Eerdmans, 1977.

Any situation which constrains our freedom tests our faith as we call out to God, 'please get me out of here!' While we pray for wisdom, wait for God to act, and explore options to improve our situation, we also have the opportunity to get to know God more deeply. Such experiences are often God's proving ground for us, part of His purpose to grow our faith and make us more like Christ.

Questions

1. Are there times when you have felt trapped in your work situation?

2. How has your Christian faith enabled you to face such situations?

3. In what ways have you experienced the freedom that Jesus Christ offers?

25. Frustrated

'At times the whole world seems to be in conspiracy to importune you with emphatic trifles.'[4]

What do you find frustrating about your daily work? Who do you get frustrated with? Sometimes it's the little things that drive us over the edge. But work often throws up some big issues too.

You may get frustrated with your bosses. They just don't support you when you are under pressure. You may think you know more than them, and could do a better job, but they don't listen to any of your good ideas, or, if they do, they claim the credit to *their* bosses without giving you a mention. You don't want to say too much in case you get fired, so instead you quietly seethe with frustration.

If you are in a management or supervisory role, you may get equally frustrated with those who report to you. Why can't they support you better? Why can't they do the job properly? Why do *you* always end up fixing the problems *they* should have fixed? Why do they go missing when there is an especially difficult problem to sort out?

Maybe you find those working alongside you are equally frustrating. It seems like they don't pull their weight. They arrive late and leave early. They are certainly not 'team players'.

You may get frustrated with the whole bureaucratic system of your organisation. You realise that despite all your ideas and efforts, the system just grinds on and you can't change it!

In fact, you may be frustrated with the whole direction of your life and a seeming failure to achieve your goals. Like a sports star frustrated by a career-ending injury, all you have worked for seems to have come to nothing.

---

4. R. W. Emerson & S. Appelbaum *Self-reliance and other essays* (Dover Publications, 1993), p. 54.

Even Jesus got frustrated …

Jesus got saddened, angry, and (I believe we can say) frustrated, with the religious leaders of His day with their nitpicking and blindness. They insisted on tithing even a minute amount of their spices, but they had 'neglected the more important matters of the law—justice, mercy and faithfulness'. He called them 'blind guides' who 'strain out a gnat and swallow a camel' (Matt. 23:23, 24).

He was frustrated by their lack of response to the grace of God: 'To what can I compare this generation? They are like children sitting in the marketplaces and calling out to others: "We played the pipe for you, and you did not dance; we sang a dirge and you did not mourn"' (Matt. 11:16-17). God, it seemed, could do no right.

Jesus was frustrated with the whole religious system of His day which had a long history of rejecting God's messengers, 'Jerusalem, Jerusalem, you who kill the prophets and stone those sent to you, how often I have longed to gather your children together, as a hen gathers her chicks under her wings, and you were not willing' (Matt. 23:37).

He was frustrated with His disciples. Even after they had spent so much time with Him, seen His miracles and heard His teaching, they still didn't quite 'get it'. When a storm broke out while they were out in a boat on the lake, they panicked. Jesus asked, 'You of little faith, why are you so afraid?' (Matt. 8:26).

Yes … even Jesus, in His short life on earth, got frustrated.

Frustration in a fallen world

Our frustration is one of the results of the fall. The first humans only had to wander round the Garden of Eden to collect all the food they needed. Afterwards, life got a whole lot more frustrating. God said to them, 'Cursed is the ground because of you; through painful toil you will eat food from it all the days of your life … By the sweat of your brow you will eat your food until you return to the ground' (Gen. 3:17-19).

Frustration will always be a part of life, and therefore part of work, in a broken world. Working with difficult, unreasonable, lazy and even cruel people is hard and frustrating. It's very frustrating dealing with the stupidity of some bureaucratic processes, unreasonable parents,

angry customers and impossible deadlines. It's frustrating when you can't seem to get anything done at home because you are looking after infant children all day.

A friend of mine was a young minister at a church in a large established denomination. He was getting worn down and depressed by all the frustrations of his new job and the heavy demands placed on him. He was challenged by an older lady, who was one of his staunchest prayer supporters. 'You shouldn't get depressed working for the Lord!' she said, trying to encourage him. 'Molly', he replied, 'it's not working for the Lord that gets me depressed ... It's working for this organisation!' This true story could be told about many other organisations, Christian and otherwise!

If you work for an organisation, secular or religious, you may find it easy to relate to that. We can start the day with the highest and best intentions, but sometimes the system and the people grind us down!

There is never a shortage of people, organisations and situations to frustrate us. But before we start to feel too sorry for ourselves, let's remember that others may find *us* even more frustrating! We're just not aware of it.

Dealing with frustration

When I find other people frustrating, I have learned that I need to pray for them, and act well towards them. Looking back, some people who I found very frustrating at first, have later become close friends, as God has given us a love and respect for each other.

When I find situations frustrating, I may need reminding that the world was not created for my convenience. It doesn't revolve around me. 'Suck it up princess, stop feeling so sorry for yourself' might be the right advice to give to ourselves here!

If our efforts have all come to nothing, or if we feel we have wasted years of our life in a dead-end job, then we can still hold on to God's promises. The Old Testament prophet Joel spoke these encouraging words to a farming community in Israel at a time when all their years of hard work had come to nothing. All the grain, fruit and vegetables they had worked so hard to produce were gone ... devoured by a plague of locusts. But God promised: '*I will repay you for the years the locusts have eaten*' (Joel 2:25).

In his long years in prison, Paul must have felt frustrated at being unable to travel to the churches he had founded and the places he had visited, frustrated by the lack of reading material and the limited companions to talk to (2 Tim. 4:9-13). In his letter to the Ephesians, he had urged them to live *making the most of every opportunity* (Eph. 5:16). Did he take his own advice? Yes! Instead of drowning in self-pity while enduring the endless hours of prison life, he did the only three things he could do in that situation. He shared the gospel with those in prison, guards and fellow prisoners; he prayed, and he wrote letters.

Two thousand years later, those letters have been translated into over 400 languages and are read by millions of Christians every day. God used a seemingly difficult, frustrating situation of a prisoner, to bless millions of people over two millennia.

When I find life frustrating, I try to remember Reinhold Niebuhr's prayer 'God grant me the serenity to accept the things I cannot change, the courage to change the things I can and wisdom to know the difference'.[5]

Questions

1. What situations and people do you find frustrating in your work?

2. How are you dealing with it?

3. How can you turn these frustrations to good in terms of your Christian life and witness?

---

5. Reinhold Niebuhr as quoted by Fred R. Shapiro, 'Who Wrote the Serenity Prayer?' *The Chronicle of Higher Education*, April 28, 2014.

26. Bored

'So my heart began to despair over all my toilsome labour under the sun' (Eccles. 2:20).

Boring work

As a student, I worked for two months stocktaking for a major car manufacturer. It was tedious in the extreme and an unbelievably inefficient and drawn out process. We were herded into a massive warehouse with hundreds of large steel bins containing vehicle parts, stacked high on shelves. The forklift truck driver would lower a bin to the ground and we would work in groups counting the number of bearings, gear levers or brake pedals in each bin. We tried to ward off the boredom by working our way through the stock bins at a fast pace. The supervisor wandered over and stood watching us. After a long silence, he muttered, 'the sooner you finish, the sooner you'll get laid off' and walked off.

We stopped and looked at one another. We all needed the money. So, we learned to play a different game. We would inexplicably lose count after nearly finishing each bin and had to start again. It was soul destroying, boring, dishonest and ethically indefensible.

Boredom is a common experience at many workplaces. Here are three more real life examples:

- You are stuck at home looking after young children or an elderly member of the family. You are doing the same jobs every day. You feel trapped, frustrated and *bored*! You resent the way that your friends' lives seem to be much more exciting than yours.

- The organisation that you work for is winding down, or about to be taken over by a larger company. There is very little productive work to do and everyone spends the time searching

for jobs on the internet, downloading music or playing computer games. There is a general atmosphere of gloom and boredom in the office.

- In your factory there has been a product recall for a safety check. You are given the job of checking 10,000 boxes for the possibility of a fault. After what seems like a very long time you look at your watch: only two hours gone and only one hundred boxes checked. 9,900 to go and six more hours of this before the end of your shift. Inside you are screaming out, 'Help! I'm bored out of my brain! Get me out of here!'

Boredom is not necessarily synonymous with repetition. Some repetitive tasks at least have an identifiable end-product, like laying bricks, painting the house or making curtains, where the worker can take some pride in the job. It's much more boring when we see no purpose in what we are doing, or when we have to perform the same manual or bureaucratic tasks over and over again. Our minds start to wander. We daydream, to 'wile away' the hours, to plan our escape from our current 'prison' to a more interesting and enjoyable place.

Each of us has a different threshold of boredom. How do we deal with it?

Dealing with boredom

'I'm bored. What can I do?' I guess many parents have heard that complaint from their children at some point, on long car journeys, shopping trips or in the school holidays. I remember a teacher who used to tell us that 'only boring people get bored!' She was probably right, but I never found that dictum particularly helpful. What was I supposed to do? But that childhood complaint about boredom may well recur through adult life. How can we 'redeem the time' to find some meaning in work that seems like drudgery?

Use of smartphones has transformed repetitious tasks. Go visit an open-plan drafting office. Most of the people will have at least one earpiece, listening to their favourite music, partly to shut out distracting noise around them and partly just to make the task more

enjoyable. On the commuter train I use, just about everyone is plugged into their smartphone or tablet on their daily journey to and from work. Smartphones don't do much to improve human interaction, but they do help relieve boredom. Doing boring tasks as part of a team at least provides opportunities to get to know workmates, and maybe to share a laugh. Clockwatching is deadly.

What does the Bible have to say about boredom? At first sight, very little! But it does have wise things to say about dealing with the many meaningless and pointless experiences we will have in the mess of this fallen world. The Old Testament book of Ecclesiastes paints a wonderfully honest picture of the pointlessness and meaninglessness of life and work without God: *'So I hated life, because the work that is done under the sun was grievous to me. All of it is meaningless, a chasing after wind'* (Eccles. 2:17). But it also offers glimpses of good news in seeing even boring, frustrating work as a gift of God: *'A person can do nothing better than to eat and drink and find satisfaction in their own toil. This too I see is from the hand of God'* (2:24). So the writer urges us, *'Whatever your hand finds to do, do it with all your might'* (Eccles. 9:10), and he ends his long reflection on the meaning of life: *'here is the conclusion of the matter: Fear God and keep his commandments, for this is the duty of all mankind'* (12:13).

We are only on this earth once. We only have this day once. If I am bored at work and can't easily change my situation, then, I can ask God to change my attitude, to open my eyes to see what I *can* do rather than focus on what I can't do. Who knows how God might use our 'boredom'.

When I am waiting for the bus or the train, stuck at an airport in bad weather, or waiting in the queue at the hospital for my name to be called, how can I fill those long hours? I can pray for people, for the relationships at work I need to improve, the creativity I might be able to bring to the job. I can spend my 'bored time' thanking God, memorising Scripture, praying for God to renew my life and open up opportunities. I can phone or text some messages of encouragement to friends.

If we are looking to relieve boredom by seeking ever more exciting and entertaining experiences, we are likely to end up dissatisfied. If we

look to make some good use of the time we spend doing 'boring tasks', we will not be so easily bored.

Questions

1. How can you live wisely, 'redeeming the time', 'making the most of every opportunity' in a boring job?

2. In those 'boring hours' who can you pray for? Who can you talk to, help or support? Does the work allow you to listen to music or talks on your smartphones that will lift and inspire you as you work?

27. Stifled Creativity

'I love creating something beautiful, it's what sustains me.'[6]

Some organisations seem intent on stifling all creativity in their work environments. The focus is on efficiency, standardisation and conformity. A Filipina friend worked on a production line in a garment factory making designer jeans. Every working hour, every day, she sewed in the zips. That was all she ever got to do. She never had the satisfaction of making a whole garment. It was a dehumanising process, which denied her any opportunity to exercise her creative gifts.

It's not just in factory production lines that creativity is stifled. Large organisations, even those who claim to value creativity, usually have strict guidelines on use of screensavers, and decoration of workspaces, and changing cubicles. Of course, there are good reasons for requiring compliance with organisational standards and corporate dress codes. But the sad side effect of the drive for uniformity, is that creativity and personal expression are stifled.

Bureaucratic organisations are notorious for stifling creativity. One manager I knew found it difficult to keep his staff because he wasn't interested in listening to their ideas. 'He never employs anyone smarter than him' was the damning indictment of one frustrated employee.

Creative people often find it difficult to fit into such government and corporate cultures. They may leave and start up their own businesses where they then exercise their entrepreneurial skills and creative energy with greater freedom. They can even dress how they like and put their favourite pictures on their screensavers!

It's a great privilege to have the opportunity to be creative in your daily work. Many very creative people face the daily test of having little opportunity to express those gifts in their work.

---

6. Words spoken by a friend who is a keen gardener.

Creativity and the Creator

God is the great Creator. The Bible opens with these words: *'In the beginning, God created the heavens and the earth.'* It goes on, *'God created mankind in his own image ... God saw all that he had made, and it was very good'* (Gen. 1:1, 27, 31).

Right from the beginning the Bible shows us God enjoying the act of creation and taking pleasure in the result. We are all created in His image, so whenever we bring creativity into our work, we reflect something of the character of God. The Scripture also tells us that God *'richly provides us with everything for our enjoyment'* (1 Tim. 6:17). He took delight in making things beautiful for us to enjoy.

So, the satisfaction and pleasure we get from creating something, and feeling good about it, comes from God. The pleasure of making something for others to enjoy comes from God. This is part of the image of God that remains in every human being. That is why we get such enjoyment in making clothes, in decorating, in building furniture, writing a book, developing a computer program, cooking a meal or in growing a business. It's why we get pleasure from seeing other people enjoy what we have created. It's how we are wired.

The Bible describes the building and furnishing of the Tent of Meeting (a mobile worship centre) by the people of Israel during their time in the wilderness. It highlights the creativity they brought to the task. Indeed, it notes specifically that the craftsmen were 'filled with the Spirit of God'. They were specially gifted for the task, by the Creator Himself.

'The Lord said to Moses, "See I have chosen Bezalel ... and I have filled him with the Spirit of God, with wisdom, with understanding, with knowledge and with all kinds of skills—to make artistic designs for work in gold, silver and bronze, to cut and set stones, to work in wood and to engage in all kinds of crafts"' (Exod. 31:1-5).

Artists, musicians, architects, gardeners and designers bring creativity to their task in quite obvious, visible or audible ways. If you decide to redecorate or refurnish a room, it may be because of the enjoyment you get in creating a different environment, as much as by a need to improve your living space. Pavement artists and sand sculptors

have their work wiped out almost every day. Their job satisfaction lies in the creative acts themselves rather than in any lasting benefits.

My wife and daughters are creative in artwork, décor and fabrics. That creativity inspires them to spend longer hours than they need to add that spark of creativity to everything they do. That in turn provides satisfaction and fulfilment beyond any financial outcome from their work.

But creativity is not just about being artistic. You may be creative in designing a simple tool for use in your workshop, in redesigning work processes and systems in your manufacturing plant or in designing computer software. You may creatively identify new business opportunities, or, you may just invent a smarter, faster, cheaper way of doing your task. Thank God for our inbuilt creative gifts. It's one of the key motivating factors to work and certainly one of the factors that makes work enjoyable. How often have you worked late without getting paid just for the satisfaction of creating something new and making it work?

If you feel that your creative gifts are stifled in your workplace, what can you do? Look for another job? Find an outlet for your creativity outside of work? Or, look for opportunities to be creative in small ways which brighten the day and give your workmates some pleasure. Most jobs provide opportunity for creativity whether it's the 'cubicle rat' decorating their workspace, the admin staff designing a screensaver, the team creatively celebrating birthdays and successes, or just being creative in your personal appearance.

If we are in any managing or supervisory role, let's be mindful of those who work for us and encourage their need to express their creative gifts. Let's not stifle creativity.

Questions

1. What opportunities do you have to be creative in your daily work?

2. How can you honour God through your creative gifts?

3. If you have responsibility for others, how can you encourage their creative gifts and abilities?

28. Pressured to Conform

'Do not conform to the pattern of this world, but be transformed by the renewing of your mind' (Rom. 12:2).

Peer pressure doesn't end with teenage years. The pressure to conform comes from all directions, at every stage of life. We are all pressured, whether overtly or subtly, to conform to the pattern of this world, to adapt our beliefs and our principles to fit the culture and the standards of the society we live in.

In some cultures that demand for conformity is particularly strong. Watch the military parades of totalitarian powers, past and present. It is a frightening view of the absolute conformity demanded by leaders with absolute power. Everyone is dressed the same, all moving the same way, at the same pace. If you take one person out, another takes their place without any noticeable difference. It is dehumanising.

Even in more democratic environments, if we work in a large organisation such as a government bureaucracy, the military, or a large corporation, we face pressure to conform, to be just another cog in the machine, to conform to their rules, regulations and dress-codes.

Most good organisations now encourage and promote diversity amongst their employees. Even so, in our day, we see increasing pressure on Christians, from large private companies as well as government organisations, to 'fit in', not to talk about their faith at work, not to express any views on issues which are contrary to the majority view, to conform to secular world views and standards, particularly on matters of gender and sexuality. In protecting one minority, it looks like our society is starting to persecute another.

In some countries, we see outright persecution and murder of Christians 'the people of the cross', who will not convert to the

dominant religion, or obey the demands of their government to suppress any public expression of their faith.

Uniformity or diversity

During our years living in Mauritius, our church met in a building with a high-pitched roof, designed to resist cyclones. The end gable wall was built from the attractive blue-black basalt rock that forms much of the island. Sitting in the service one day, I noticed that every rock had been hand-placed, and every rock had a different shape. By contrast, in the house next door, every brick looked the same. They had been mass-produced to be the same shape and size. This picture has remained in my memory as a contrast between the uniqueness of the human beings created by God and the conformity demanded by many human societies.

Humans do mass-production and often resort to pressuring people to conform to majority beliefs and behaviours, to be just 'another brick in the wall'. God creates individuals and diversity, not uniformity (see for example Ps. 139 and Eph. 4). I am suspicious of any organisation that enforces uniformity to the point of not valuing the individual contribution. It smacks of power play, self-aggrandisement and domination.

The call to be different

The call to *be* different in the best possible way, and to *live* distinctively different from non-believers, comes right through the Bible. John Stott makes the point that 'the first characteristic of the radical disciple is non-conformity.'[7] Stott reminds us that this foundational theme recurs throughout the Bible:

- In the Law: '*You must not do as they do in Egypt, where you used to live, and you must not do as they do in the land of Canaan where I am bringing you. Do not follow their practices.*' (Lev. 18:3);

- In the Prophets: God confronts His people: '*... you have not followed my decrees or kept my laws, but you have conformed to the standards of the nations around you*' (Ezek. 11:12);

---

7. John Stott, *The Radical Disciple* (IVP, 2013), pp. 20-21.

- In the Gospels: Jesus points to the religious hypocrites and warns His disciples *'Do not be like them'* (Matt. 6:8);

- In the New Testament letters: Paul says, *'Do not conform to the pattern of this world, but be transformed by the renewing of your mind'* (Rom. 12:2).

To be different, means you stand out from the crowd. That may bring us into conflict with the powers that demand uniformity to the point where we cannot, in good conscience, comply.

Way back in the days of the Babylonian Empire, the Jewish exiles came under increasing pressure to conform. King Nebuchadnezzar demanded that all his followers bow down and worship him. Shadrach, Meshach and Abednego refused and were thrown into a furnace from which God miraculously delivered them.

Dictators throughout history have gone down this same path, demanding worship rather than just respect for their office. The early Christians faced enormous pressure to conform to the dictates of the Roman Emperor, to declare publicly that 'Caesar is Lord'. Those who refused, who asserted that Jesus is Lord, i.e., more powerful than Caesar, faced the death penalty.

We are seeing similar pressures on Christians in many totalitarian societies today.

Making a difference

But 'being different' is much more than just taking a stand against something we don't agree with. Jesus calls us to make a difference for good.

Jesus and His followers were pressured to conform in a different way by the religious leaders of their day … *'Why do you eat and drink with tax collectors and sinners?'* (Luke 5:30). The implied criticism was, 'Why aren't you like us and do what we do?' But Jesus showed a quality of care for unloved people that put to shame the pious hypocrisy of the religious elite.

We can either be like a thermometer or like a thermostat. A thermometer simply measures the temperature of its environment. A thermostat sets the temperature, rather than merely adapting to it.

In our community and our workplace, do we set the standard or simply adapt to the accepted norms? To use the biblical analogies (Matt. 5:13-16), are we like salt arresting decay, or have we lost our saltiness? Are we like a light, shining in the darkness, or has our light practically gone out?[8]

Last year, I visited Sicily, and toured the ancient site at Agrigento. To my surprise, in the midst of the ruined temples, I discovered 'The Garden of the Righteous'. It was a low-key modern memorial, but to me more impressive than the ancient ruins. It stopped me in my tracks. It was dedicated to those who had died in recent times making a stand against the Mafia. One small plaque was dedicated to Piersanti Mattarella with this inscription:

> 'To be remembered for his Christian behavior. A man who loved justice. He was killed by the Mafia for his love of the beauty of human and divine law.'

It is a beautifully worded tribute to a politician who sought to raise the bar of morality in dealings between business, politicians and the bureaucracy. He made his stand and paid with his life.

Questions

1. In what ways are you pressured to conform to values and behaviours that are contrary to your Christian beliefs?

2. How have you handled these situations?

3. When and how do you need to make a stand?

---

8. See Graham Hooper, *A Better way to live* (Acorn Press, 2015), p. 2.

29. Aimless

'We make it our goal to please him ...' (2 Cor. 5:9)

A colleague described his life as like 'a road to somewhere'—moving on but with no clear destination and no real direction. Perhaps you feel like that right now. Aimlessly wandering. Maybe you have lost your way. You still hold on to Christian faith, but you have no sense of God's purpose for your life. In the daily pressures of surviving life at work, it's easy to lose our sense of direction.

Marketing people speak of the 'elevator pitch'. If you had thirty seconds, riding in an elevator with a potential customer, to explain why they should buy your product rather than another, or why the employer should award *you* the job rather than the other person, what would you say? It's a good test to see how clearly we understand our own message. If you had thirty seconds to explain to someone *what your life is for*, what would you say? Try it.

Organisations use different terms to define what they hope to achieve. Some speak of having a *vision* (meaning here a clear end in mind rather than a mystical experience), or a *mission*, or simply clear *goals and objectives*. All are designed to express the collective thinking and harness the collective energy in a common purpose.

Sometimes we need to pause, press the reset button and get a new fix on our direction in life, to get a clear vision of God's purpose in our work, a sense of mission and some clear objectives.

Vision

Visions inspire and motivate. Jesus had a clear vision of what lay beyond His death. It was *'for the joy set before him he endured the cross ...'* (Heb. 12:2). The early Christians had a vision, like that of Abraham who *'was looking forward to the city with foundations, whose*

architect and builder is God' (Heb. 11:10). They were on a journey and they 'saw the goal' ahead of them.

The leaders of the civil rights movement of the 1950s and 60s in America had a vision when they sang 'keep your eyes on the prize and hold on'.

The Christian's ultimate vision is to *'be with Christ'* (Phil. 1:23). That is what motivated the Apostle Paul to keep doing what he was doing. When we lose sight of that, we lose hope. We lose direction and forget what is important and valuable. Work becomes drudgery—just a necessary evil.

By contrast, having a clear vision of where we are ultimately heading, motivates us to live and work wherever God leads us.

Mission

All great mission statements are simple. Christ explained His mission, the purpose of His life on earth, in one of the simplest, but most profound theological statements ever made: ... *'the Son of man came to seek and to save the lost'* (Luke 19:10).

Jesus also left us with a number of clear mission statements to provide the framework for the life of every Christian in every age and in every culture: to love God and love our neighbour (Mark 12:30,31), to be faithful (Matt. 25:23) and to be witnesses to Him (Acts 1:8).

Goals

Goals are specific objectives. Jesus had specific objectives during His mission on earth. He knew that He would have to go to Jerusalem to die (John 12:27). He had a clear view of why He was on earth. It was to do the will of His Father (John 6:38). He came to do the works of the One who sent Him (John 9:4). He came to serve and to give His life as a ransom for many (Mark 10:45). Jesus' goals were perfectly aligned with those of God His Father.

Mission statements for organisations help align and focus objectives and channel collective energies. Personal mission statements and goals may similarly help focus our thinking and channel our energy.

Re-setting direction

If you feel you have lost direction, then why not try getting clear in your mind, and perhaps writing down if that helps, what you believe your purpose is in life, what direction you are taking, what goals you hope to achieve and what decisions you need to make. But at the same time, let's remember that living and working as a Christian is not a matter of us formulating our personal goals and then asking God to help us achieve them. It's about understanding what God has revealed in the Bible about *His* goals for this world, and for our lives, and then fitting into that.

God is sovereign over our lives and circumstances. What we believe to be our mission or goal may well get changed by God in His love and wisdom. I am writing this in the midst of the Covid-19 pandemic. Over six million people have died so far. Many more have lost their jobs and had their plans disrupted in the compulsory lockdowns as life is reduced to the basics. It's a stark reminder that we do not control as much as we think; perhaps a timely wake up call to remember that we are here on earth to do the will of God and honour Him, not primarily to achieve our personal goals. It is also a great opportunity to re-set direction.

A colleague expressed his personal 'mission statement' like this: 'to demonstrate the reality of God in the way I live and work and to reflect the character of Christ in the way I conduct myself and deal with people'. Others think in terms of a series of commitments.

- to love my marriage partner and be faithful to my vows
- to *be* the best that I can be
- to *do* the best that I can do
- to be a consistent witness to Jesus Christ.

However we think about our future, we would surely be wise to pray, 'Lord, help me to understand *your* purpose for my life and help me to fulfil it with the gifts and abilities you have given me, and show me *your* priorities for my life'.

Questions

1. What do you believe is your purpose on this earth? Try putting it into your own words.

2. What specific goals do you have in your life? What goals do you have in your work? Have you brought these prayerfully to God?

3. If you feel you have lost direction in life, what *one thing* can you do right now to make a step forward?

30. Envious

'Envy: a feeling of discontented or resentful longing aroused by someone else's possessions, qualities or luck.' OXFORD DICTIONARY

Are you content, or do you have a gnawing anxiety that others are getting a better deal, having life easier, achieving more, or having more fun than you? We can easily find ourselves gripped by envy and a fear that others are succeeding when we fail. It's the 'FOMO' factor—fear of missing out.

FOMO feeds off social media. Jenny posts some selfies on Instagram, photos of herself relaxing with a glass of wine on a tropical island while you are slaving away at the office and struggling to pay the rent. Andy posts his daily blogs of his backpacking adventures through South America, which you read while sandwiched on the morning commuter train. Your find yourself envious and irritated at the same time. There is also a twinge of self-doubt, 'Am I missing out on life's best?'

Do you find yourself thinking like this?

'I don't have as much money as ... X'

'I don't have such a good job as ... X'

'I don't live in as big a house or have as good a car as ... X'

'I don't go on overseas holidays like ... X'

As we look around at our workmates, we might ask ourselves 'Why does the boss praise her and not me? Why don't I get invited to the team lunches? Why did he get the pay rise and not me?' Apart from breaking the tenth commandment, 'you shall not covet', all these doubts and fears rob us of the peace of God and enjoyment of our relationship with God.

When promotions and special appointments are up for grabs, when thanks and awards are announced, and you miss out because someone

else is preferred instead of you, how do you feel? When someone else gets the credit for your ideas, leadership and hard work, how do you react?

Abi was a young schoolteacher who, together with an older colleague, was given the responsibility of putting on a special children's show for the parents. Nearly all the ideas and energy came from the younger teacher, but, at the end of the performance, when the head teacher was handing out the accolades, it was the older teacher who was given all the credit. It was hard to take.

The attractive alternative

What are the antidotes to envy? Thankfulness, and a settled order of priorities leading to contentment, are a good start.

Thankfulness

One of the features of sin is that we always want more. However wealthy we are, we always think we will be a little bit happier if we had just a little bit more. Our definition of 'rich' usually means 'someone with more than me'. Envy and anxiety are symptoms of having no peace with God and being discontent with ourselves. Back in the Garden of Eden, Adam had just about everything, but he wanted more.

A work colleague refused to get drawn into coffee room gossip and grumbles about pay. When asked how much he was getting paid, he used to reply 'Enough'! Thankfulness to God is a great antidote to anxiety and 'FOMO'.

Priorities[9]

Being clear on what is important to us also helps us overcome envy and fear of missing out. The psalmist made his priorities clear like this: *'I would rather be a doorkeeper in the house of my God than dwell in the tents of the wicked'* (84:10). The psalmist knew what his priorities were. He had proved in his own experience that he was most content when he was living and working in the presence of God.

Jesus said: *'Seek first his (God's) kingdom and his righteousness and all these things (the things we worry about and strive for) will be given to you as well'* (Matt. 6:33 … my comments in parentheses).

---

9. See also chapter 15.

The challenge for each of us is simple: will we trust God, or will we be anxious and envious that others are doing better and getting more?

Contentment

I have a book at home, written by Jeremiah Burroughs, a seventeenth-century English Puritan, entitled, *The Rare Jewel of Christian Contentment*. The title tells a story in itself. Contentment is indeed a rare and precious thing.

Our ideal picture of contentment may involve relaxing with a cool drink and a good book, or a quiet rest after a tiring day, but such feelings of 'contentment' may quickly pass. One phone call from a troubled friend or member of the family quickly breaks the spell. The Bible paints a picture of a deeper and different kind of contentment, an inner sense of 'shalom'. This peace comes from knowing God loves and accepts us and being thankful for what God has provided, rather than always grasping for more:

> 'But godliness with contentment is great gain. For we brought nothing into the world, and we can take nothing out of it. But if we have food and clothing, we will be content with that' (1 Tim. 6:6-8).

A friend, who held a management position in a large business, was informed by her boss that a new role was being established, and a new person had been recruited to lead the department. As my friend had spent years successfully building up her department and growing the business, her first reaction was anger. Why had she been overlooked after performing so well? Why should she now have to report to someone else? It was so unfair. She realised, that at the root of her anger was envy. It gnawed away at her for several weeks. Her pride had been hurt. She felt belittled in front of her colleagues when the new appointment was made public. She then entered a second phase of reactions which involved letting others know how badly she had been treated. Her anger, anxiety and envy spilled over into destructive behaviour. Openly she co-operated with her new boss, but she was no longer giving the job her best and no longer enjoyed her work. As she prayed, she had to confess her wrong attitude as a Christian and to trust that God knew what was best for her. She had to learn all over again what it meant to do her work

'for the Lord', to give it her best and respect her new boss. As she did so, the whole atmosphere gradually changed, and my friend's reputation was actually enhanced, as others recognised how well she had handled herself in the process. She came through this difficult period in her working life, and this testing experience for her Christian faith, both stronger and wiser and as a good witness to Jesus Christ.[10]

Questions

1. What makes you envious in the workplace?
2. What can you give thanks for in terms of your work, your finances, and all that God has blessed you with?
3. What are your priorities?

---

10. Graham Hooper, *Undivided—closing the faith life gap* (Inter-Varsity Press, 2013), p. 90.

31. Setbacks

'Do not gloat over me my enemy! Though I have fallen I will rise. Though I sit in darkness the Lord will be my light' (Micah 7:8).

When you finished your studies at school, college or university, I wonder how you pictured your future. Perhaps you envisaged a steadily rising line of increasing success, more money and a greater sense of personal fulfilment.

The reality, as you look back, might be more like a profile of a mountain range with hills and valleys, high points and lows. The likelihood is that you will have setbacks and disappointments at some point. If you haven't had this experience in your life so far, then you must be living in a bubble. It may well burst sometime soon!

Setbacks at work often look (and feel) like failure. We may fail because of our own moral weakness: we behave inappropriately or do something dishonest and let ourselves and our family down. We may fail due to our own stupidity; fail the exam because we haven't studied, fail to get the job because we haven't prepared for the interview or fail in our work because we haven't given it our best. We may fail because we are just not as good as the competition. We've worked hard and long, but we still don't get the job, the contract, or the promotion.

But some setbacks are due to adverse circumstances entirely beyond our control. Some major event like a flood or fire may destroy all we have worked for and leave us asking 'Why?' Sometimes life is like that.

How do you cope with setbacks like that? I guess it depends to some extent on your personality and on your mood and circumstances at the time. Sometimes we can shrug them off, redouble our efforts, look forward and press on. At other times, setbacks hit us like a body blow, leaving scars which take a long time to heal.

'Setbacks' beyond our control

King David, the Old Testament hero, experienced some low points that must have seemed like 'failures' but which were due to events outside his control; persecution from King Saul, the death of his great friend Jonathan and the pain and humiliation of having his own son (Absalom) turn against him.

On one occasion, he hit rock bottom (1 Sam. 30:1-20). He was on the run from Saul. His days of court popularity after his conquest of Goliath were long past. He gathered a band of men around him and lived as a fugitive. While he and his men were away, a marauding band burned their camp to the ground and carried off the women and children and all their possessions. The Scripture tells us that '*David and his men wept aloud until they had no strength left to weep*' (30:4). Then, the situation went from bad to worse. The men started looking for someone to blame. They turned on David and threatened to kill him.

Whenever I read that story I try to imagine how David felt. This was not his fault. The circumstances were beyond his control. Everything seemed to be going wrong for him. David seemed to have failed totally to achieve what he wanted to achieve. He was an anointed king, but with no kingdom, a soldier, now seemingly defeated, a leader who had lost the support of his men, a man who had lost his possessions and a husband and father who had failed to protect his family. Now, he was in danger for his life.

Then, the Scripture says: '*David found strength in the Lord his God*' (30:6). He was alone, and yet he found strength in the Lord to face the situation. The story goes on to tell how he rallied his men; how they went out and recovered their families and possessions and turned a massive setback into total victory.

Recovery

When you and I face real discouragement in situations at work; when things go badly wrong, when we feel alone with no one to turn to, what do we do? If we learn one thing from David's experience, we learn how to find strength in the Lord our God as the first step in recovering from failure. This was all a long time ago in a different culture. But there is a timeless truth here. When life looks very dark, with no light at the end of the tunnel, when our faith is tested to the limit, God is still

there, and His promises are still good. He will strengthen us to face the difficulties; He can turn our setbacks into successes, in His way, and in His time. It's that waiting for God to act that tests and grows our faith.

I can think of a number of setbacks in my working life, when I have come home feeling utterly depressed, but how in God's time, new opportunities emerged that I *had not foreseen*. What looked for a while like failure was turned around. Looking back, the experiences themselves are still painful, but I can thank God for what I have learned and thank Him for bringing me through those dark times.

Let me share with you seven steps forward, in recovering from setbacks and failures, that I have learned in my working life.[11]

1. Rediscover your value in the sight of God: according to the Bible, the value of our life, is NOT measured by what we have achieved, by our wealth, title, qualifications and status in society. Rather it is the value God has put on our life in giving His Son for us. That is the value that lasts.

2. Focus on Jesus Christ, on His great love for you, rather than focusing only on yourself and your setbacks: The Bible calls us to consider Him, to learn from Him, to be rooted and grounded in Him, to remain in Him, to please Him.

3. Do one thing well, some act of service, take a step forward, rather than dwell on the past. Who knows what small thing or what single act may be much more important in the sight of God than our most treasured achievements?

4. Resist the temptation to succumb to envy, jealousy and bitterness, but rather be thankful. Thankfulness is a very attractive quality … envy and jealousy are not.

5. Invest time in relationships: learn to value people above things and even above achievements.

6. Hold on and don't give up trusting that God has a great plan for you. Failures test our faith and resilience and are often a stepping-stone into a better future.

7. Press on and take whatever opportunities are open to you.

---

11. Hooper, *Undivided*.

Questions

1. What 'setbacks' have you experienced in your work?

2. How have you recovered from them?

3. What have you learned about God and yourself in the process?

32. Redundant

'I was made redundant from my first job in advertising. The reality of it was that I didn't know how I was going to pay the rent. But one thing I did sense was an underlying peace that came from a knowledge that God doesn't get taken by surprise.' [12]

Let me share three true stories. [13]

- Andrew was a mechanic in the automotive manufacturing industry. His role was to solve difficult problems in the production process. He was called into his boss' office on a pretext of another meeting and summarily dismissed along with several others. It was a typical 10 per cent downsizing exercise by a major corporate. He didn't see this coming and he felt shattered. It took several months to deal with the deep feeling of failure and rejection, of being unwanted and unvalued, as he searched for a new direction in his life.

- Lisa, a marketing executive with a large corporation, received two letters, each from a different division of the organisation, within two days. The first advised her that she had been appointed to a new role (good news!), the second informed her that her whole division had been closed down and her services were no longer required (bad news!). You can imagine her reaction.

- Peter was a Project Manager working as an expatriate in the Middle East for a company which claimed 'integrity' and 'people' to be two of their five core values. He was married. His children were students in a local high school. A week

---

12. 'Redundancy', The Graduate Alphabet, Fusion UK, 2013.
13. I have changed the names of those involved to respect privacy.

before Christmas, he received a phone call from his North American office to say that he and the other six members of his group were 'being terminated'. The company was cutting costs and their group was the first casualty. What could he do? He had very little chance of even looking for a new job: most companies were preparing for their Christmas/New Year closedown. None of the decision-makers were available to deal with job applications. Should he cancel the lease on his apartment? Should he take his children out of school? If so, where to? That particular story ended happily. Some colleagues helped him find another job in the same location, but it didn't work out so well for the others made 'redundant' that day.

In the industrial heartlands of North America and Europe, many communities bear the scars of big industries closing down, as the businesses have become non-viable and manufacturing uncompetitive compared with lower cost competitors. The human cost is enormous: high unemployment, alcohol and drug problems, marriage breakdown, domestic violence and divided communities, as people struggle to find work and feel unwanted.

The term 'redundant' is itself a dehumanising word when applied to people. It means surplus to requirements, no longer needed. To be fired, made redundant, 'retrenched' is a hard blow to anyone's self-esteem. For someone who has taken great pride in their work over a long period, to stand in the queue at the Job Centre can be a humbling and humiliating experience. It is usually also a very anxious experience. How will I face my friends? How will I pay my bills?

Biblical perspective

The Bible has some powerful things to say to us when we are really down. Often, it's only in the difficult and dark times that we discover that they are not religious platitudes, they really are God's Word to us, big truths to hold on to and to rely on. Here are some of them:

- God does not stop loving us or wanting the best for us (Rom. 5:8). His love does not change with our work situation.

- God is Sovereign over our lives. He is in control. Our situation is not going to take Him by surprise. We can look to Him to guide us in our next step (Prov. 3:5-6).

- God does not promise us a steady upward path of material success in this life. Faith in Christ is not an automatic entry ticket to a world of prosperity. Losing our job, or being unable to find work, may be the difficult path we have to tread for a while as we learn to rely more on God and less on ourselves (John 16:33).

- God may bring us through 'wilderness experiences' like redundancy, failure at work, or failure to get a job. He may test us and humble us and teach us lessons about ourselves and about the faithfulness of God; lessons that we may not learn any other way (Deut. 8:2).

Only twelve miles to Elim … a personal story

I was in my early thirties. We were in the UK, staying with my wife's parents, with our two young children and baby, all in one room. I had been offered a job in Australia and we were waiting for our visa to come through. After a three-month wait, our morale was at a low ebb. Every day the neighbour enquired whether we had heard. Every day we had to reply in the negative. I started to avoid him because I didn't want to have to admit to having no job and having to rely on my in-laws for housing. Then I was notified that the job offer in Australia had fallen through. I was shattered … no job, no other prospects in the pipeline and rapidly declining savings. That Sunday in the local church, the minister spoke on the Exodus story, the journey of the Israelites through the wilderness. He focused on this passage:

> 'Then Moses led Israel from the Red Sea and they went into the desert of Shur. For three days they traveled in the desert without finding water. When they came to Marah, they could not drink it because it was bitter … So the people grumbled against Moses, saying, "What are we to drink?" …. There the LORD issued a ruling and instruction for them and put them to the test … Then they came to Elim where there were twelve

springs and seventy palm trees, and they camped there near the water' (Exod. 15:22-27).

When the people arrived at Marah to find the water was undrinkable, it was the last straw. They had lost faith in Moses and lost faith in God. But God miraculously made the water drinkable, and He told them to keep trusting and obeying Him. They pressed on. After only twelve more miles, they arrived at the oasis of Elim where there was plenty of food and water.

The message was simple. Hold on and keep trusting. God will provide for you. It was a Word from God to me. The very next day, we received a long communication from my prospective employer apologising for a mistake. They had meant to say that though the original post no longer existed, there *was* a job there for me, albeit a different one to that originally offered. Within four weeks we were on the flight to Sydney. It was a test of faith. Life seemed bitter when the job fell through, but God led us on to our 'Elim'.

Bad experiences, like being made redundant or unable to find work, are always easier to look back on than to go through. Maybe you are going through a testing time of having lost your job or having no job right now. It is a real test of faith. 'Is God still there? Is He still there for me? Does my faith only work in the good times?' Yes, yes and no are the Bible's answers to those three questions. We can lean all our weight on Him. Keep trusting that God will work the hard experiences to good and that He will bring you through into a good place.

Questions

1. What experiences of testing through redundancy or difficulty in finding work can you look back on?

2. What did you learn about God and about yourself in the process?

3. What help can you give to someone who has just lost their job or who can't find work?

33. Stressed

'When hard pressed, I cried to the Lord; he brought me into a spacious place' (Ps. 118:5).

The problem

Workplace stress takes a heavy toll. It impacts business in terms of lost productivity, but the human toll is harder to measure. It's a huge mental health problem. Workplace stress affects everybody. It affects workers' health and enjoyment of life. It also affects their families and relationships outside of work.

I have left this chapter to last in this part of the book because stress has many different causes and manifestations. In the last few chapters, we have looked at testing experiences like frustration, boredom, and envy. In Part 2 of the book, we looked at difficult relationships, unreasonably demanding bosses, bullying, harassment, conflict and exploitation. All are major causes of stress at work.

Stresses and strains

I am not a medical doctor, nor a psychologist, so let me tread carefully here and stick to what I know. I first learned about stress and strain in high school physics lessons. Stress is force applied per unit area. Strain is elongation per unit length. Put simply, there is push and pull.

These basic principles of physics translate well into everyday human experience. We instinctively understand what is meant by 'stress and strain'. We say we are *stressed* when we feel pressure, internal or external. When the stress is too much for us to withstand, we say we feel 'crushed' under the load. Similarly we experience *strain*. We speak of being 'pulled in too many directions at once', of being 'stretched to our limit', or 'close to breaking point'.

We can take this analogy further. Some materials are more elastic than others. That is they can withstand stress and strain and quickly

revert back to their original condition. Rubber is elastic. Plasticine, on the other hand is inelastic; it doesn't recover its original shape when the load is removed.

As with different materials, we all have a different ability to withstand stress and strain. It varies according to our physical and mental make-up, our personality, our health, mood, and our situation. In 'normal' healthy times we might be able to handle stress and recover quickly. At other times, for example after a major trauma, stress can leave a lasting and damaging impact which is not easily reversed. Those suffering with PTSD (Post Traumatic Stress Disorder) know that only too well.

Knowing ourselves

'Know thyself' was one of the three maxims inscribed at the entrance to the Temple of Apollo at Delphi in Ancient Greece. The late Dr Martin Lloyd Jones, former physician and Christian minister, used to frequently emphasise the importance of 'knowing ourselves'. In his classic book on Spiritual Depression he wrote: *'The main art in the matter of spiritual living is to know how to handle yourself.'*[14] I believe what 'the Doctor' wrote about depression also holds true for stress. We need to understand our strengths and weaknesses, physically and emotionally, and how we are likely to think, act and react when we are stressed at work.

One of my daughters has type 1 diabetes. She has learned that stress at work plays havoc with her sugar levels and can seriously damage her health. She has learned how to manage that stress and heed the warning signs her body sends her.

We all need to know how far we can push ourselves and still bounce back for more. When do we need to dig in and say 'No! I just can't take that on'? When do we need some down time and exercise, or just enjoy a day off?

We are all wired differently. At work, I usually function more efficiently with the stress of deadlines. It must be a hangover from my habit of last-minute cramming for exams as a student! The adrenaline flows, and I work better.

---

14. Dr Martin Lloyd Jones, *Spiritual Depression: Its causes and cures* (Pickering & Inglis Ltd., 1965), p. 20.

But each of us needs to understand how best to deal with our stress. My late father used to enjoy walking and gardening for relaxation. Some like to chill out with a good book or a movie. One of my sons-in-law burns off his work stress with a long bike ride, the other by playing competitive 'Ultimate-Frisbee'. Some leisure activities can be very stressful, but the stress is different. In my student days I used to enjoy rock climbing. I dealt with the stress of exams by escaping at regular intervals into a different world of clinging to a cliff face where the only decision I had to make was the next upward move. In its own way it was wonderfully relaxing. As Ryken observed, *'Many (leisure) activities require effort and are even physically or mentally strenuous, but they are experienced as leisure because they are freely chosen and carry the rewards of leisure.'*[15]

I recently took an exercise stress test in which the doctor intentionally put my heart under stress to see how it performed. When we are stress-tested at work, we will certainly learn more about ourselves. I suspect that the more we know ourselves, the better we are likely to handle stress.

Knowing those we work with

We also need to understand those we work with and how they function under stress. That's part of our responsibility to care for one another. Most people I have worked with like just enough stress to make work interesting and challenging, but not so much as to cause anxiety, panic or depression.

Some people can be loaded up with work, perform well to tight deadlines and come back every day ready for more. Others will have a sleepless night about a seemingly small task like organising the morning coffees. We need to learn to recognise signs of stress in those we work with.

But there are a whole range of factors in play here. Our workmates may be stressed at work for a wide range of reasons that have nothing to do with the work itself. Do they have sick children at home? Are they struggling with a relationship breakdown, elderly parents with dementia, money worries, or are they just trying to juggle too many things at once?

---

15. Leland Ryken, *Work and Leisure in Christian perspective*, (Wipf and Stock Publishers, May 2002), p. 32.

When we deal with stressed-out people, it's all too easy to resort to platitudes: 'slow down', 'take it easy', 'don't worry', 'don't work so hard,' 'don't sweat the small stuff'. All said maybe with good intent, but not really helpful in dealing with their problem. The least we can do is to listen, try to understand, and help where we can.

Some biblical insights

Stress is not glossed over in the Bible. Indeed, we see some of the Bible 'heroes' acting under severe stress. David was relentlessly and unjustly pursued by Saul who wanted to kill him. Later, he feigned madness to escape his enemies (1 Sam. 21). Elijah, emotionally drained after a major confrontation with the Queen's false prophets on Mount Carmel, sat alone in the desert and wanting to die; *'I have had enough Lord, Take my life ...'* (1 Kings 19:4).

Paul describes the stress he experienced, *'We are hard pressed on every side, but not crushed; perplexed, but not in despair; persecuted, but not abandoned; struck down, but not destroyed'* (2 Cor. 4:8-9). On top of all his physical suffering and hardships, he carried a load of heavy responsibility: *'Besides everything else, I face daily the pressure of my concern for all the churches'* (2 Cor. 11:28).

In stressful times I like to turn to the psalms, particularly those written under intense pressure and by people struggling to hold on to their faith in the midst of it.[16] Above all we can turn to the Lord Himself, who made us and who, in Christ, shared our humanness. Jesus experienced stress beyond our understanding in the Garden of Gethsemane when *'his sweat was like drops of blood falling to the ground'* (Luke 22:44). He it is who offers us a rest and peace which He alone can give.

Jesus would often take time out on His own, to get away to lonely places to think and to pray (Mark 1:35; Luke 4:42). If Jesus needed to do that, how much more do we?

Questions

1. What is the main cause of stress in your life? How do you deal with it?

2. In what ways is stress a positive in your work?

---

16. See for example, Psalms 3, 13, 88, 119,

PART E

KEEPING FOCUSED ... ON 'THE BIG PICTURE'

> 'He knows the way that I take. When he has tested me, I will
> come forth as gold' (Job 23:10).

I love mountain climbing. I love the satisfaction of standing at the summit and looking round with a 360-degree view. It's inspiring and invigorating. It would be nice if we could always have that same 'mountain-top' view of the value and purpose of our lives and our work in the sight of God, to be confident that we are doing something worthwhile and somehow playing a part in the outworking of God's plan for His world. Even better would be to understand what God is doing when we are right in the middle of testing situations. We might long to have that mountain-top view, but sometimes our daily experience feels more like thrashing around in dense jungle looking for the path.

In this final section, let's look 'above the clouds', at the big picture, by asking some questions. They are questions that I have asked myself, and tried to answer, at various times in my working life:

- Why would the great God who made the universe, and who keeps it all running, be interested in my work?

- What is the value of our work in the light of eternity? What is ultimately worthwhile?

- How much is my worth as a person tied up with what I do and achieve?

- How do I know if I am in the right job?

- What is God calling me to do?

- What does it mean in God's eyes to 'succeed' in my work?

- What 'legacy' will we leave behind?

Being a Christian is a lifelong learning experience. Some of the answers to these questions that I have learned, and go on learning, are fleshed out in the next few chapters. Of course, only God knows all the answers, but He has revealed to us enough to guide us and encourage us along the way (Deut. 29:29).

34. God at Work

'God is working his purpose out as year succeeds to year.' [1]

A different perspective

I was driving home through the city traffic after a particularly frustrating day. I was having a conversation in my head with a difficult client, going over the problems. In my mind, I was letting loose all my frustration and saying the things I would like to have said, but (thankfully) didn't. Then I remembered that I was due to speak in church the following Sunday and I needed to focus on that. I started to wonder: how were these two things linked in God's eyes? Frustration at work on Friday ... church on Sunday? Was I being a total hypocrite in standing up in front of others with my Bible and unconsciously conveying an impression that I had life under control?

Then, sitting in the car I had what you might call a 'mountain-top moment'. Not in the sense of some ecstatic experience, but just in seeing clearly what seems blindingly obvious when I now write it down. It was ALL part of God's work in my life. He is at work always, not just when I remember to ask Him, and not just in the good times. More than that, I was so wrapped up in *myself* and *my* perspective on things, I started to remember that God cared about the other people I worked with. He cared about the organisation I worked for. I needed to pray for my boss, my workmates and for their families, for God's work in their lives, not just go over and over my own problems. In this sinful, stressful world of course such moments of clarity may be few and far between. But when they come, they can be life changing and memorable.

I learned a life lesson. As we try to understand the significance of our daily work, let's remember that it's *not* just a matter of what *we*

---

1. Arthur Campbell Ainger, 1894.

do, why *we* do it, and how *we* do it. There is a bigger picture. Work has eternal significance because of what God is doing. He is a worker and He is always 'working His purpose out'.

So it's not a matter of us making our plans, setting our work goals and asking God to bless them and give us success. It's not about fitting God into *our* agenda. It's about us committing to serving God in and through our work and asking Him to use us in *His* plan.

God is at work in His world. We can do our work expecting to see God at work answering prayers, transforming difficult situations in our home ... workshop ... factory ... office ... school ... hospital ... building site ... laboratory, wherever. We can pray, 'Lord, this is your place. You have put me here'.

Some workplaces are particularly 'toxic'. When we have to deal with all the hassles and bad stuff that goes on, it can feel like being sent out into enemy territory. In a sense we have, but we need to remember that the same Lord we worshipped in church on Sunday is present with us at work on Monday morning. Jesus said, *'I am with you always, to the very end of the age'* (Matt. 28:20). I have found that it's good to remember that, at the beginning of each day, travelling in the train or bus, or as we start work at home.

God may be at work in the lives of those we work with. That is always exciting to experience. I once shared an office with a colleague who came to faith in Christ over a period of months. I can't recall how it happened. I don't remember any critical conversations or life-changing moments. But, like Lydia in the New Testament (Acts 16:14) the Lord opened his heart. It was a great encouragement to me to keep praying for my workmates and to build relationships with them. We can go to work expecting to see God change people's lives.

God is at work in us. According to the Bible, God's plan for us is to change us into the likeness of Jesus Christ. He gives us His Holy Spirit to live in us, to change us and to give us strength to do what we would not otherwise be able to do. It's not about 'self-improvement' or 'self-fulfilment', it's about God-transformation. As Paul wrote: *'Continue to work out your salvation with fear and trembling, for it is God who works in you to will and to act in order to fulfill his good purpose'* (Phil. 2:12, 13). It is often in the pressure cooker of work, in

the rough and tumble of life, that God works in us and moulds us into the people He wants us to be.

God may choose to work through us, in changing the whole atmosphere and culture of our workplace, in helping others, and even in bringing others to know Him. A friend of mine worked in a manufacturing plant which employed over 400 people. I asked him what lessons he had learned as a Christian in his work. His reply: 'Never underestimate the power and unconscious effect of people committed to doing their job "for the Lord", compared with those just working for their pay. There were only three other committed Christians in our factory: the Maintenance Foreman, the boss' PA and the Production Manager. This was the real strength of the business. It was those three people who held the whole operation together. Things were never the same after they left.'

God is not just engaged in our lives and in our work situations when we choose to pray to Him. He is always there. He is always at work.

A view from the top

Perhaps we need to lift our eyes away from ourselves and our work problems for a moment to see the bigger picture and consider the amazing plan of God for His world. Paul's letter to the Ephesians, sometimes called 'the Alps of the New Testament' is a good place to turn to:

> *'In him (Christ) we have redemption through his blood, the forgiveness of sins, in accordance with the riches of God's grace that he lavished on us. With all wisdom and understanding, he made known to us the mystery of his will according to his good pleasure, which he purposed in Christ, to be put into effect when the times will have reached their fulfillment—to bring unity to all things in heaven and on earth together under Christ'* (Eph. 1:7-10).

This is a breathtaking overview of God's plan for His world, everything united under the rule of Jesus Christ. So how do we fit into this grand plan? Paul goes on; *'by grace you have been saved through faith—and this is not from yourselves, it is the gift of God—not by works, so that no*

one can boast. For we are God's handiwork, created in Christ Jesus to do *good works which God prepared in advance for us to do'* (Eph. 2:8-10).

I find this wonderfully encouraging. God, in His grace, has worked in our lives in bringing us to faith in Jesus Christ. He continues to work in us. He will even use us to do the good things He has prepared for us to do. He includes us in His plans—that is a big picture worth contemplating!

Questions

1. What difficult situations are you facing in your work right now?

2. What changes in attitude and behaviour do you think God wants to make in your life?

3. What people in your circle of contacts at work can you start praying for … to see God at work in their lives?

35. Not in Vain

'Always give yourself fully to the work of the Lord because you know that your labour in the Lord is not in vain' (1 Cor. 15:58).

Most of us ask ourselves at one time or another during our working lives, 'Why am I doing this?' Consider these real-life stories.

- The marketing team prepare a major tender; they work for several weeks, working long hours into the night, giving their creative best. The tenders go in. They lose. They ask themselves, 'What was *that* all about?'

- The technician gives thirty years of loyal service to a family-owned food company. The firm is sold to a multinational. He is fired three months after the takeover. He is left feeling bitter and asking, 'What price loyalty?'

- The group in the government department is instructed to prepare a report on a major social issue. They consult widely with the community and spend months drafting and redrafting their report, but their political bosses have now moved on to other issues. The report is filed and never read. What was the point?

- The counsellor patiently spends hours and hours with a young offender, seeking to break the repeated pattern of drugs, violence and crime. The young person re-offends and is sent back to prison. Was the whole process a waste of time?

- The farmer invests his savings in equipment and materials to plant his crop of wheat. He works long and hard, ploughing, and planting. But there is no rain. His reservoir of water dries up, making irrigation impossible. He loses the crop and goes deeper in debt to the bank. All his effort seemed to be in vain.

- A thirty-six-year-old infrastructure manager admits to having spent fifteen years of his life being discontent. He had worked for years on a huge water treatment plant which had been mothballed by the government, and then on a tunnel that he felt the city did not need. He seemed to spend his life (he said) in arguments with bureaucrats, lawyers and financiers. What value was there in all that effort?

The book of Ecclesiastes paints a picture of a very successful business leader, with great possessions who, after a career of great achievements, sadly concludes, '... *when I surveyed all that my hands had done and what I had toiled to achieve, everything was meaningless, a chasing after the wind ...*' (Eccles. 2:11).

So, what meaning does *my* work have in the context of eternity? The equipment I repair, the report I write, the structures I build, the meetings I attend, the dishes I wash? What value do they have in God's eyes? Are we destined to look back on our working lives and feel we have missed God's plan for our lives; that our life path has been 'second best', or conclude that it was all meaningless? A waste of time? In vain?

The promise of fulfilment

The Old Testament prophet Amos was given a vision of the blessing that God will bring to His people. He expresses it in beautiful poetic language like this: '*They will plant vineyards and drink their wine, they will make gardens and eat their fruit*' (Amos 9:14). In other words, the workers will no longer be alienated from the product of their labour. Rather, they will enjoy the fruits of their hard work. All the digging and planting, watering, fertilising and pruning will be worthwhile. Their work will not be in vain.

The prophet Isaiah, in his vision of the new heaven and new earth, saw God's people enjoying life in God's new creation, including the blessing of purposeful, fruitful work: '*They will not labour in vain ... for they will be a people blessed by the LORD*' (Isa. 65:23).

The Christian has the privilege of looking forward to this great future and also to enjoying a foretaste of that experience now. When Paul wrote to the Corinthians about the resurrection of Jesus, and the assurance that death will not have the last word for the believer,

he concludes on a high note, '*Where O Death is your victory, where O Death is your sting … thanks be to God! He gives us the victory through our Lord Jesus Christ*' (1 Cor. 15:55-57).

Then he does what the Bible so often does. He gets us to think about our life on this earth in the context of the afterlife. He earths wonderfully inspiring teaching back into the nitty gritty of the here and now, and presents a view of life and work which is strong and purposeful. He writes, '*Therefore, my dear brothers and sisters, stand firm. Let nothing move you. Always give yourself fully to the work of the Lord, because you know that your labour in the Lord is not in vain*' (v. 58).

What does Paul mean here by 'the work of the Lord' that is not 'in vain'? Is he referring to overtly 'Christian work?' Some would say yes[2]. Paul means the work of evangelism, discipling and growing churches. As we look at this verse in the context of the whole letter that seems to be the obvious conclusion (see, for example, 3:1; 9:1 and 16:10).

But, if that were true, then for those of us who have day jobs in the secular world, what is the value of the work we do? Is it some sort of spiritual limbo land; just an infill between Sundays; just a means of supporting ourselves and our families; a necessary evil we have to make the best of? In terms of value, is it all a second-best use of time for the Christian or, worse still, something ultimately meaningless, of no spiritual value … time and effort spent in vain?

The Bible's answer to those questions is a resounding NO! Paul says, '*Always give yourself to the work of the Lord*' … **Always!!** I quoted earlier in this book these two famous instructions to the Christians at Colossae: '*Whatever you do, whether in word or deed, do it all in the name of the Lord Jesus, giving thanks to God the Father through him*' (Col. 3:17); and, '*Whatever you do, work at it with all your heart as working for the Lord, not for human masters …*' (3:23).

Note the all-inclusiveness of both these instructions: 'whatever you do …' that surely includes all of life, not just the obviously religious bits.

---

2. E.g. C. K. Barrett 'So what is meant in these passages is the Christian labour of calling the church into being and building it up,' 1 Corinthians, *Blacks New Testament Commentaries*, p. 385.

The takeaway from all this? Our work, whatever it is, done in the name of Jesus and for Him, is never in vain. It has an eternal purpose and will have a fruitful outcome.

Questions

1. What does it mean in your workplace to '*work at it with all your heart as working for the Lord?*'

2. What satisfaction do you get from your daily work?

36. Identity and Worth

'For someone who has good reason to believe that he doesn't exist apart from what he does, to doubt that he has done anything worthwhile is to gaze into the abyss.' CLIVE JAMES[3]

Identity

Is 'who we are' defined by what we do? If our self-esteem and our sense of identity is based on our work, and on the respect we earn through our work, then what happens when we retire, or lose our job, or start to question its value?

At a work function some years ago I met a former senior executive of a large company who had just retired. He introduced himself with the words: 'Hello, I'm Bill, I used to be somebody ...' He was half-joking but, in the way he said it, he was unintentionally revealing his struggle with the loss of the position of power and respect he had once held. That had gone, and with it a chunk of his own self-esteem. It was clear that he felt the loss of a part of his identity now that he was 'just a retiree' rather than the head of a large company.[4]

When I shared that story with a retiree recently, he responded with a smile. 'I get that,' he said, 'I used to run a plant and equipment business of 400 people. Now I just manage my backyard'.

A young woman who had recently exchanged her executive role for full time motherhood told a similar story. 'I used to travel a lot and deal with interesting people. Now I change nappies and clean up the chaos at home!'

It's hard when we move from a position in which we feel valued and respected, to one in which there is no one concerned about what *we*

---

3. Clive James, *May week was in June* (Jonathan Cape Ltd., 1990), p. 239.

4. See *Undivided*, p. 91.

think and no one wanting our advice. It lays bare the whole question of our sense of identity and self-worth.

A friend of mine in his mid-30s suffered 'burnout' from the pressure of work. He described his change of attitude as he slowly recovered like this: 'I started to see myself more as a human *being* and less of a human *doing*'.

Value

Picture yourself at a job interview, trying to explain to a future employer your potential value to the organisation. What do you say? We usually submit a resume which sets out:

- Our qualifications—how clever we are

- Our skills—what we can do

- Our personal attributes, what a good person we are: honest, hardworking, passionate, team player etc.

- Our experience—what we have done successfully

- Our potential to add value to our employer

In other words, we pitch a value proposition about our worth. It's very different when we approach God. We come into this world with no assets, and we leave in the same state. We don't come to God with a summary of good reasons why He should accept us, a track record of behaviour and accomplishments. No. We come with empty hands to receive His grace. That applies to the President as much as to the cleaner, to the CEO as to the factory worker.

So how would you put a value on your worth as a person? How would you measure it?

- the total value of your assets?

- your future potential earnings?

- the value you add to the organisation you work for?

- your ability to inspire others through your leadership?

- the wealth you leave behind when you die?

These would be the most common ways of assigning financial value to individuals. But the best measure of worth, of a company being sold, or of anything we possess, is what someone is willing to pay. We might think our apartment is worth a certain amount, but when we put it on the market, we find the best offer we get is way below that figure. Conversely, we might discover a dusty old painting in our grandparents' attic that is worth a fortune when it goes to auction.

True value

Jesus said that the value of our life in God's eyes is not the sum total of our assets, *'Life does not consist in an abundance of possessions'* (Luke 12:15); nor our future potential, nor even what we contribute or don't contribute to society; it is the price He was willing to pay.

He paid what He thought we were worth. He paid with His life. That is the value God has set on our life, whatever we achieve or fail to achieve. In the words of the Apostle Peter, *'For you know that it was not with perishable things such as silver or gold that you were redeemed ... but with the precious blood of Christ'* (1 Pet. 1:18, 19). We are worth something because Christ paid the price of His own life for us. There is nothing we need to do, and nothing we can do, to prove our worth to God.

In emphasising our value in the eyes of God, the Bible makes much of our new identity when we put our trust in Christ. We are a new creation in Christ (2 Cor. 5:17). We belong to Him (1 Cor. 6:19-20). We are adopted into the family with God as our Father (Gal. 4:6-7).

If we carry this biblical understanding of our worth and identity into our daily work, then we will have the right attitude. It will free us from so much anxiety that results from valuing ourselves by our own perspective on our status or achievements.

Valuing others

As we remind ourselves that God does not assess our value by our assets, skills and achievements, we can easily fall into the trap of dismissively valuing others by similar measures—'she is a waste of space—he is a complete loser, etc.' Who are we to treat as worthless those whom God created and for whom Christ died?

A medical doctor shared with me this lesson she learned about valuing other people:

> 'When I was a junior doctor on the wards of a major hospital, a young man was admitted under our unit. He had taken an overdose of Panadol and his liver was shot. I summarised his case to the professor by offering my opinion that I did not feel he should be referred to the special liver transplant unit because, well, he didn't deserve it. After all, he was a druggie—read, undeserving, scum of the earth—and we could save precious healthcare resources! My professor did not agree with me. He said that this patient was only a young man, with his whole life ahead of him. I instantly felt rebuked that I, a Christian, did not have the grace to see this man as a human being deserving of compassion and a second chance that a liver transplant might give him! I have never forgotten that incident.'

God has set a value on every life. He made us all. Christ died for all.

Questions

1. In what ways do you consciously or unconsciously value other people?

2. How do you value yourself?

3. What needs to change in your attitudes to others and to yourself in the light of the gospel?

37. The Right Work?

'Godly work is good work, done in a godly way for God, for His glory, and in His strength ... the most mundane action can carry the fragrance of Christ' MARK GREENE.[5]

In any honest conversation with Christian people about faith and work, especially young people who are just starting work, these two questions usually come up. *'What work should I be doing?' 'Is there work a Christian should not do?'*

I have found that I need to pause and breathe a silent prayer for wisdom to avoid launching into a 'pat answer'. What lies behind the questions? Is the questioner trapped in a job where they are having to compromise their values? Does she feel that she could be doing something more satisfying and more useful? Is she looking for a short-cut, a 'set of rules to follow' rather than seeking God's guidance for herself?

The Bible doesn't lay down hard rules about what work we should or shouldn't do, though some try to make up the rules for us! It is, under God, a matter of conscience, so people will come up with different answers.

For example, I know pacifists who can't accept that any Christian should fight in the armed forces. But I also know, as you may, godly Christian men and women in the military for whom this is their calling and daily work.

We had an ex-convict in our church who had become a Christian while serving a long jail sentence for assault and robbery. When he came to faith in Christ, he found it hard at first to accept that any member of the police force could be a Christian. He had spent his whole life hating the police. He reached a turning point when he was asked

---

5. Mark Greene, *Fruitfulness on the frontline* (IVP, 2014), pp. 92 and 94.

to tell his life story to a Christian Police Officer's conference! In the process he discovered many new friends and enjoyed the unexpected experience of Christian fellowship with people he had once regarded as his enemies.

If you have strong views about alcohol, you might think that no Christian should work in a brewery, a bar or hotel. If you see the entertainment industry as a cesspit of evil, then you will find it difficult to accept that Christians should work in that industry. What about business? I hear a lot of old jokes about whether we will meet any lawyers, politicians, investment bankers, etc., in heaven! But there are many Christians in the hospitality industry, many actors and singers and producers who seek to honour God through their work, and of course there are Christian lawyers, politicians and bankers as there are Christians in almost all walks of life. As in all matters of conscience, we are unwise to be too dogmatic or judgmental.

Where exactly we draw the line will vary. But we do need to decide where we stand so that we can go out and do our work in faith, for the Lord and in His name.

Working differently

As John the Baptist talked to the people about the coming Messiah, and warned them about God's coming judgment, the people were convicted. They asked him how they should change their lives. *'Tax collectors came to be baptized. "Teacher," they asked, "What should we do?" "Don't collect any more than you are required to," he told them. Then some soldiers asked him, "And what should we do?" He replied, "Don't extort money and don't accuse people falsely—be content with your pay"'* (Luke 3:12-14).

Tax collectors worked for the occupying Roman forces. They were given free licence to exploit the people by charging more than the imperial tax and pocketing the difference. Notice that John did *not* tell them to get a different job. Rather he told them to do their job differently. Neither did he tell the soldiers to leave their job. He did tell them to stop abusing their power to make money for themselves.

God's call to us is not necessarily to do different work, but rather to do our work differently, in a way that honours the name of Christ.

A matter of conscience

In Paul's letter to the Romans he gives guidance to Christians who are arguing about matters of conscience. In Paul's time, the debate was about certain foods that Christians should or should not eat, or special days they should observe. The principles he lays down in dealing with these 'disputable matters' are timeless and have wider application to other matters of conscience.

First, he warns us not to judge one another: *'Who are you to judge someone else's servant? To their own master, servants stand or fall'* (Rom. 14:4).

Then he counsels us to pray about our choices in these matters and to keep a clear conscience before God: *'So whatever you believe about these things, keep between yourself and God. Blessed is the one who does not condemn himself by what he approves ...'* and, *'everything that does not come from faith is sin'* (14:22, 23).

So, applying these principles to our daily work, we might ask ourselves:

- Can I do what I do with a clear conscience?

- Is what I am doing going to build people up or bring them down?

- Can I do what I do 'in the Name of Christ', consistent with His teaching and character?

If we can say yes to those questions, then we are 'doing good work' whatever our actual task. It is the Lord Christ we are serving.

Richard Baxter, a Puritan pastor, gave this wise advice way back in the seventeenth century: 'Choose that employment or calling in which you may be most serviceable to God. Choose not that in which you may be most rich or honourable in the world; but that in which you may do most good and best escape sinning.'[6]

Questions

1. What is it you really want in your work? What is really bugging you? Is it that you are not paid enough, not valued enough,

---

6. 'A Christian Directory', Richard Baxter *Printed by Robert White for Nevill Simmons, 1673. Early English Books Online Text Creation Partnership, 2011.*

not stretched enough? What is making you dissatisfied? What is it that you really need … a change of attitude, or a change of job, or both?

2. Are you trying to find something in your work and career, a satisfaction that can only be found in a relationship with God through Christ? A successful career without God is still going to leave you feeling empty.

3. What needs to change in your own attitudes and behaviour?

38. Career or Calling?

'You also are among those who are called to belong to Jesus Christ' (Rom. 1:6).

'Careers used to be like railway trains. You get on at the station and ride them to the end of the line. Now they're more like cross-county terrain vehicles.' That comment was made to me by the Human Resources Manager of a large company. He had been in the business for over thirty years and was reflecting on the trend away from long-term careers with a single organisation to a much more flexible situation with people changing jobs and employers every few years.

I was invited to the retirement party of a senior government official. He had spent his whole working life with one department, posted to various locations around the country. He summed up his experience like this: 'I've lived in thirty-five different houses, driven twenty different cars, done fifteen different jobs, had five dogs, three children ... and one wife.' He added, 'Looking back, I think I got those things in the right proportions!'

He had what we might call a 'distinguished career'. Most people in this world don't have that luxury. My late father worked for forty-eight years for Dunlop. He lived through two world wars and a devastating economic depression. He didn't think in terms of a career. He was happy just to have a job. But for those who do have the privilege of thinking about their future in term of progressive career development, let's reflect on how that fits with biblical teaching on work.

It came as a surprise to me to discover that the Bible has no concept of a *career*. It focuses more on God's call and on serving Him and others in response to that call. A career is all about *you*, what you want to do and be, where you want to go and how you plan to get there. A calling is all about God and His will for your life. A 'calling'

comes from God. Your career is planned by you. As Leland Ryken observes, 'There can be little doubt that one of the problems with work in our day is an overly individualistic work ethic … "What's in it for me?"'[7]

The concept of a career, and of career planning, derives from the massive increase in opportunities opened up to the educated middle classes in the nineteenth and twentieth centuries in societies in which such opportunities flourished. Prior to that, the majority had little choice. They worked on farms, in cottage industry, domestic service to the rich, military service or, post-industrial revolution, recruited for the mines and factories. Educated middle-class males had choices which were generally denied to females. They might become a doctor, an officer in the military, a banker, financier or city trader of some sort. The more adventurous ones might venture overseas to set up a farm or a business. The working classes, like the great majority of workers worldwide today, had very limited choices.

God's call

If you are a Christian, it is because God has called you. Somewhere deep in your spirit, you heard the call of God and responded. That call of God may come to us in different ways:

- As a command from Jesus, *'Come follow me'* (Mark 1:17).
- As an invitation from Jesus: *'Come to me all you who are weary and burdened, and I will give you rest'* (Matt. 11:28).
- As a growing conviction, like Lydia *'whose heart the Lord opened'* (Acts 16:14).

What does He call us to? He calls us to change the whole direction of our life. Jesus said, *'I have not come to call the righteous but sinners'* (Matt. 9:13). He calls us out of darkness and into light (1 Pet. 2:9), to freedom (Gal. 5:13) and into the fellowship of His Son (1 Cor. 1:9).

When Paul wrote to the Church of Corinth, he addressed these ordinary working people as *'called to be his holy people, together with all those everywhere who call on the name of our Lord Jesus Christ'*

---

7. Ryken, p. 172.

(1 Cor. 1:2). This is the Christian's *general* calling; it applies to every Christian, whatever their job. It's not just for a few especially religious people. It's a call from the Lord, by the Lord, to the Lord.

God may also call us to a particular role, to exercise a particular gift or to work in a particular place. There are several references in the New Testament which seem to indicate strongly that God has prepared specific tasks for us to do for Him (e.g. Eph. 2:10).

So, how do we know what we are meant to be doing at any point in time? Under God, the answer to that question lies in understanding and embracing our particular mix of gifts, education, desires, opportunity and inner conviction.

I have spent my life working in the infrastructure business. I can't say I have ever experienced a supernatural call to do what I have done, more an inner conviction about the path I should follow. This has led to opportunities to use my abilities in my work. Looking back, I can see how God has led me. I have sometimes known the prompting of the Spirit of God and the challenge of the Word of God to new things. I am very thankful for the friends I have made, and for the opportunities to serve through my work, wherever my job has taken me. I also thank God for the testing experiences that have stretched my faith and deepened my understanding of God. For me, it has been a case of praying for God's guidance and then just going through each door as it opened, rather than intentionally working out where I wanted to go, and how that would help 'my career'.

Of course, that process has not always been straightforward. God may lead us through many testing situations on the way, (including those we have considered in this book). We have to learn to trust Him when His guidance does not seem clear. Sometimes it seems like we go down 'dead end' paths. We don't necessarily get the perfect job. There may be limited opportunities in the field we want to work in, or we don't have high enough qualifications. I have met many highly educated people driving taxis because they couldn't find any opportunity to use their skills and training. We may sometimes find ourselves having to earn our daily bread doing work we would rather not be doing, or having no paid job at all.

Whatever our situation, we are called to belong to Christ and to serve Christ in our daily task, using the gifts God has given us. That

task may change several times in a lifetime from student to trainee, to employee, to homemaker, to business owner, to full-time carer to voluntary worker, before finally 'retiring' and finding a new role! We may have multiple 'callings' at the same time; for example, to be a wife, a mother, a manager, a volunteer helper, a group leader at church. God may call us to work in a particular location or in a particular way of serving at home. Are we open to His call on our lives?

Rather than asking ourselves 'am I missing my calling?' or 'what is my vocation?', perhaps we would do better to ask, 'how can I serve God in my current situation?' The Bible's focus seems to be that whatever our job, we are called to do it as an act of service for God. We are not meant to live in a constant state of anxiety about whether we are missing our true calling. Rather we are to get on with our work, doing it for the Lord. He will make it clear if He wants to call us to do something else.

The New Testament often uses the picture of the Christian life as a race: not a sprint, but more like a marathon. God has a race for each of us to run. We all have the same finishing post, the same guide and companion, but your race is different to mine. You may wish you had someone else's rather than your own, but God has entrusted *you* with a set of work responsibilities and family situations in which to live out your life, as a Christian. He gives us this encouragement:

> '... let us throw off everything that hinders, and the sin that so easily entangles. And let us run with perseverance the race marked out for us fixing our eyes on Jesus the pioneer and perfecter of our faith' (Heb. 12:1-2).

Questions

1. What difference would it make to your life to see your daily work as a calling from God?

2. In what ways do you serve others in your daily work?

39. Measuring Success

'Well done, good and faithful servant!' (Matt. 25:23).

'Jim has worked for forty years, but he has nothing to show for it.' That was the dismissive comment made by a work colleague about a mutual friend who was nearing retirement with very little in the way of savings. The man in question had actually enjoyed an adventurous life. He had a loving family and was looking forward to working less and enjoying more leisure time.

When our time comes to look back on our working life, what will we have to show for it? What will we value most? Our retirement savings or our family? Our accomplishments or our relationships? Our big house or the satisfaction of knowing and serving God?

What will you take into retirement in terms of memories, friendships, or frustrated ambition? How will you measure whether your life has been 'successful'?

We usually define success in terms of finishing a task, completing a course or winning a competition. Success in our world is mainly about getting, winning and achieving. It's also about *the way* we, compete, achieve and accrue. Even in a materialistic, success-driven culture, the business people and politicians who bribe their way to the top, or the athletes who cheat by using banned substances, are not considered 'successful'.

Success is a relative measure. If you are an elite sportsperson, then losing the grand final may look to you like failure, but to most others, just to compete in the finals would be seen as an outstanding achievement. We might succeed in one particular area of life and fall badly short in others. You may succeed in business but have disastrous personal relationships, or the other way around.

The Bible doesn't speak much about success. It gives us other criteria by which to assess our life: blessing, fruitfulness, fulfilment, and faithfulness.

Blessing

'Success' is a very human-centred concept. We tend to see it as the result of *our* effort, *our* abilities and *our* commitment. The Bible gives us a God-centred view. We may say 'that woman has been a great success'. The Bible would say, 'She has been greatly blessed'. This famous prayer of Aaron expresses God's blessing like this:

> *'The LORD bless you and keep you; the LORD make his face shine on you and be gracious to you; the LORD turn his face toward you and give you peace'* (Num. 6:22-24).

Experiencing God's blessing is like knowing the smile of God on your life.

Psalm 1 paints a beautiful picture from nature of a person blessed by God, *'That person is like a tree planted by streams of water, which yields its fruit in season and whose leaf does not wither—whatever they do prospers'* (Ps. 1:3).[8]

Fruitfulness

God intends us to be fruitful. He works in us to produce the fruit of the Holy Spirit *'love, joy, peace, forbearance, kindness, goodness, faithfulness, gentleness and self-control'* (Gal. 5:22). He works through us to make a difference for good in the world. Fruitfulness produced by the Holy Spirit will also lead to others coming to faith in Christ and being built up in that faith. This is the 'fruitful labour', which Paul referred to in his letter to the church at Philippi (Phil. 1:22).

The apple tree in my garden produces a lot of fruit, but none of it lasts. Some gets taken by birds, some falls to the ground and rots and some gets picked and eaten! By contrast, Jesus promised that the fruit He produces by His Spirit in our lives will last ... forever (John 15:16).

---

8. See also Psalm 84 for a description of one who is blessed by God: they focus on praise and worship of God (v. 4), they live as pilgrims (v. 5), and go from strength to strength.

Fulfilment

'I have never felt so fulfilled in my work.' Those words were spoken to me, not by the leader of a great organisation, but by a woman working for low pay, serving in her local community. Fulfilment can be an elusive experience. Like happiness and success, it doesn't come by seeking it as an end in itself, but as a by-product of something bigger. The insightful prayer of St Francis highlights the truth that ultimate satisfaction comes from giving rather than getting:

> 'O Divine Master, grant that I may not so much seek
> to be consoled as to console;
> to be understood as to understand;
> to be loved as to love.
> For it is in giving that we receive;
> it is in pardoning that we are pardoned;
> and it is in dying that we are born to eternal life.'

Fulfilment is the sense of being complete, of being in the right place at the right time and in using the gifts we have been given. Fulfilment comes from service, rather than selfishness.

Faithfulness

According to the Bible, success is also about being faithful to God, in our relationships and in our daily work (see also Chap.10). It is about doing the will of God and looking forward to hearing the Lord say to us: *'Well done, good and faithful servant! You have been faithful with a few things I will put you in charge of many things. Come and share your master's happiness'* (Matt. 25:21)

Blessing, fruitfulness, fulfilment, and faithfulness—that's the view of success God sets before us in the Bible. Why settle for lesser alternatives that can never satisfy?

Looking back, looking forward

One of the saddest phrases in the Bible is found in Psalm 78 where the writer looks back to the failure of the children of Israel to trust God. Instead they wandered round the desert for forty years, going nowhere, and *'ended their days in futility'* (Ps. 78:33). You may know people who have fallen into the trap of bitterness and resentment, of becoming

'grumpy old men' and 'grumpy old women'. They had a dream once, for a better life, but it hasn't been fulfilled. They feel cheated, and they 'end their days in futility'.

It is sometimes a sad experience meeting with retirees, even those who have had successful careers, but who feel that now the best is behind them. Ahead lies old age, with its increasingly restricted opportunities and deteriorating health, and at the end … death.

By stark contrast, for the Christian believer, the best is always ahead. The Apostle Paul who was executed in a Roman prison, left few, if any, material assets but he looked back on his life with thankfulness and a sense of fulfilment. He also looked forward with hope and joy of what lay beyond the grave: *'I have fought the good fight, I have finished the race, I have kept the faith. Now there is in store for me the crown of righteousness, which the Lord, the righteous Judge will award to me on that day—and not only to me, but also to all who have longed for his appearing'* (2 Tim. 4:7-8).

Questions

1. What success do you crave?

2. Are you in danger of getting things out of proportion; of chasing after wealth, power and recognition at the expense of honouring God?

3. When 'success' comes, do you thank God and give credit to others who made it possible, or do you try to make yourself the centre of attention?

40. Leaving a Legacy

'Tychicus ... a dear brother ... and fellow servant' (Col. 4:7).

What will people say about us when we are gone? How will we be remembered? Perhaps it's just as well that we won't be there to find out. What if they say, 'The awkward old xxxxx has gone at last!'?

Many people approaching later years get very focused on what kind of 'legacy' they will leave behind. They want to be remembered by something constructive they have done in leaving the world a better place. Politicians typically want their name on a piece of infrastructure, a commemorative stone ... 'opened by ...'. or, they feel compelled to write their memoirs to record for posterity the great things they have done for the country.

Wealthy people, who have spent their lives making money, endow universities, colleges, schools or hospitals, libraries, or art galleries. They want to give something back and feel they have contributed something to the world as well as taking from it.

The head of a global bank was asked, after announcing his retirement, what he would like to be remembered for. The interviewer was clearly interested in the legacy he would leave behind in terms of his efforts in restructuring the company and improving its profitability and growth. But surprisingly, he replied: 'I want to be remembered with affection by my children; in this business I'll be forgotten in a week.' He may have been over-modest, but he had his feet firmly on the ground.

I'm not sure that God wants us to worry overmuch about the legacy we leave behind. He just calls us to concentrate on running the race set before us and living and working faithfully to the end.

Bible epitaphs

If you *are* concerned about how you will be remembered, and what your loved ones will write on your gravestone, then you might

aspire to one of these four wonderful accolades found in the New Testament.

'She did what she could' (Mark 14:8)

Jesus spoke these words to a critical group of religious people who had watched a woman anoint Jesus' head with very expensive perfume, an act of love and great respect. Those watching were critical of the waste. 'The money could have been given to the poor', they said, but Jesus turned on these carping critics with these words:

> "'Leave her alone," said Jesus. "Why are you bothering her? She has done a beautiful thing to me .... She did what she could. She poured perfume on my body beforehand to prepare for my burial. Truly I tell you, wherever the gospel is preached throughout the world, what she has done will also be told in memory of her'" (Mark 14:6-9).

Think about Jesus' words, 'she did what she could'. Nobody can do more. As Jesus foretold 2,000 years ago, this woman's legacy has lasted .... It is still being remembered all around the world. You and I are remembering it now.

(David) 'served God's purpose in his own generation ...' (Acts 13:36)

This comment by Paul about David, the hero/king of the Old Testament, was made almost in passing, in a speech to the Jewish Synagogue at Pisidian. But it tells us much about David.

He served *God's purpose* .... Despite his many obvious failings, he served the purposes of God rather than his own agenda. Further he served God *in his own generation*. That is all any of us can do ... to run the race set before us, to make the most of every opportunity in the culture, time and place in which God has placed us.

'... good and faithful servant' (Matt. 25:21, 23)

This was the commendation of the boss given to the faithful servant, in Jesus' parable of the talents. God has given us all, in varying measures, abilities, opportunities and resources and calls us to account for how we use them.

A leading Christian politician, speaking about all the pressures of public life, said 'what we all have to remember is that ultimately there is only one person to please .... God. We want to hear Him say to us "Well done good and faithful servant"'.

'... the world was not worthy of them.' (Heb. 11:38)

This last one is about suffering. It comes in the list which comprises 'the hall of fame' of people of faith in the New Testament letter to the Hebrews. The author illustrates his theme of living by faith in the God we cannot see, by referring to those who have done great things for God (11:17-33) and to those who had suffered great things for God (11:34-38). Let's note very carefully that this highest accolade in all the Bible is not reserved for the great achievers, but for those who have suffered for their faith.

Let's also notice that the common theme in all these accolades is service. As the late English Bible scholar T. W. Manson commented, *'In the kingdom of God, service is not a stepping stone to nobility. It is nobility.'*[9]

Questions

1. How would you like to be remembered?

2. As you reflect on how quickly life passes by, how do your values need to change? How do your attitudes to work need to change?

---

9. T. W. Manson, *The Church's Ministry* (Hodder & Stoughton, 1948), p. 27.

Bibliography

Augustine, *On the Sermon on the Mount*, trans. William Findlay, 1888

Baxter, Richard, *A Christian Directory*

Bakan, Joel, *The Corporation* (Constable, 2004)

Barrett, C. K., *First Epistle to the Corinthians* (Blacks New Testament commentaries, second Edition 1994)

Best, Ernest, *Ephesians: a shorter commentary* (T &T Clark, Edinburgh, 1993)

Bruce, F. F., *The Apostle of the Heart Set Free* (William B Eerdmans, 1993)

Calvin, John, *Commentaries on the Four Last Books of Moses*, Vol 1 (W. M. B. Eerdmans Publishing Company, 1950)

Calvin, John, *Institutes of the Christian Religion* 1:1:2, pp. 35-37

Chapman, Alister, *Godly Ambition: John Stott and the Evangelical Movement* (Oxford University Press, 2012)

Daley, J., *Great Speeches by African Americans* (Dover Publications 2006)

Emerson, R. W. and Appelbaum, S., *Self-reliance and Other Essays* (Dover Publications, 1993)

Flanagan, Kieran, and Gregory, Dan, *Selfish Scared and Stupid* (Wrightbooks, 2014)

Forrester, W. R., *Christian Vocation* (New York, Charles Scribner's Sons, 1953)

'Global Estimates of Modern Slavery,' ILO, 2017

Greene, Mark, *Fruitfulness on the Frontline* (IVP, 2014)

Hill, Alexander, *Just Business* (IVP, second edition, 2008)

Hooper, Graham, *Undivided: Closing the faith life gap* (Inter-Varsity Press, 2013)

Jackson, Thomas, ed, *The Works of John Wesley*, 1872 edition

James, Clive, *May Week was in June* (Jonathan Cape Ltd., 1990)

Keller, Tim, *Every Good Endeavour* (Hodder & Stoughton, 2012)

Laird, Andrew, *Under Pressure* (City Bible Forum, 2017)

Lamb, Jonathan, *Integrity* (IVP, 2006)

Lewis, C. S., *Mere Christianity* (Harper Collins, 1952)

'Loneliness and its impact on the American Workplace' CIGNA, March 2020

Mackay, Hugh, *Australia Reimagined—towards a more compassionate less anxious society* (Macmillan, 2018)

Manson, T. W., *The Church's Ministry* (Hodder & Stoughton, 1948)

Martin, Kara, *Workship* (Graceworks, 2017)

Morris, Leon, *The Epistle of Paul to the Thessalonians* (IVP, 1956)

Motyer, Alec, *The Prophecy of Isaiah* (IVP, 1993)

Motyer, J. A., *Psalms by the Day* (Christian Focus Publications, 2016)

Murdoch, Iris, *The Black Prince* (London: Chattop and Windus, 1973)

New Bible Dictionary, Third Edition (IVP, 1996)

Payne, Tony, *The Thing Is* (Matthiasmedia, 2013)

'Royal Commission into Misconduct in the Banking, Superannuation and Financial Services Industry' Final report, February 2019

Ryken, Leland, *Work and Leisure in Christian Perspective* (Wipf and Stock publishers, 2002)

Smith, Gregory S., *The Testing of God's Sons* (B&H Publishing Group, 2014)

Stott, John, *The Radical Disciple* (IVP, 2010)

'The Graduate Alphabet,' Fusion UK, 2013

'The Inner Ring,' C. S. Lewis, Memorial Lecture at King's College, University of London, 1944

Appendix

The biblical language of 'testing' and 'proving'

In my early thirties, I had the great privilege of studying Old Testament Hebrew (most of which I have sadly forgotten) for two years under the late Alec Motyer. Alec used to say frequently, 'Bible words have Bible meanings. You don't have to be a great language scholar—just sit down with your Bible and Young's concordance and see how the words are used in context. You can learn a lot'.

Following Alec's wise advice, I have listed below the main occurrences of the words used in our English Bibles for testing and proving and have drawn on many of these references in this book. The verbs most commonly used are: test, try, tempt, prove, examine, probe, refine; and the nouns: trial, testing and temptation. I have grouped these under the particular Hebrew (OT) or Greek (NT) words used in the original to help better understand the intended meaning of the words.

You might enjoy checking these out for yourself using your Bible and Young's concordance!

OLD TESTAMENT ... Hebrew words
bachan, nasah, tsaraph

Uses of *'bachan'* and derivatives

Genesis 42:15: 'And this is how you will be <u>tested</u> ...' (KJV 'hereby shall ye be proved ...')

1 Chronicles 29:17: ... 'I know my God that you <u>test</u> the heart and are pleased with integrity ...'

Job 23:10: 'When he has <u>tested</u> me, I will come forth as gold'

Psalm 7:9: … 'You the righteous God who <u>probes</u> (tries) minds and hearts'

Psalm 11:4,5: … 'He observes everyone on earth. His eyes <u>examine</u> them. The LORD <u>examines</u> the righteous'

Psalm 81:7: 'I <u>tested</u> you at the waters of Meribah …'

Psalm 95:9: '…where your ancestors <u>tested</u> me; they tried me though they had seen what I did'

Psalm 139:23: 'Search me God and know my heart; <u>test</u> me and know my anxious thoughts'

Proverbs 17:3: 'the crucible for silver and the furnace for gold, but the LORD <u>tests</u> the heart'

Jeremiah 6:27: 'I have made you a <u>tester</u> of metals and my people the ore, that you may observe and <u>test</u> their ways'

Jeremiah 9:7: 'see I will refine and <u>test</u> them, for what else can I do because of the sin of my people'

Jeremiah 11:20: 'But you, Lord Almighty, judge righteously and <u>test</u> the heart and mind …'

Jeremiah 12:3: 'Yet you know me LORD; you see me and <u>test</u> my thoughts about you.'

Jeremiah 20:12: 'LORD Almighty you who examine the righteous and <u>probe</u> the heart and mind …'

Uses of *nasah* and derivatives

Genesis 22:1: ' Some time later God <u>tested</u> Abraham …'

Exodus 15:26: 'There the LORD issued a ruling and instruction for them and put them to the <u>test</u>.'

Exodus 16:4: 'In this way I will <u>test</u> them to see if they follow my instructions …'

Exodus 20:20: 'Do not be afraid. God has come to <u>test</u> you so that the fear of God will be with you to keep you from sinning.'

Deuteronomy 8:2: 'Remember how the LORD your God led you all the way in the wilderness these forty years, to humble and <u>test</u> you, in order to know what was in your heart …'

Deuteronomy 8:16: 'He gave you manna to eat ... to humble and <u>test</u> you so that in the end it might go well with you.'

Deuteronomy 13:3: 'You must not listen to the words of that prophet or dreamer, The LORD your God is <u>testing</u> you to find out whether you love him with all your heart and with all your soul.'

Deuteronomy 33:8: 'About Levi ...he said You <u>tested</u> him at Massah...'

Judges 2:22: 'I will use them to <u>test</u> Israel ...' See also Judges 3:1 and 3:4

2 Chronicles 32:31: (about Hezekiah) 'God left him to <u>test</u> him and to know everything that was in his heart.'

Uses of *tsaraph* and derivatives

Note: occurs thirty-five times in the Old Testament, mainly in the prophets and the Book of Psalms (Expository Dictionary of the Old Testament, (Thomas Nelson Publishers 1980), p. 424)

Judges 7:4: 'I will <u>thin them out for you</u> there.'

Psalm 105:19: 'till the word of the LORD <u>proved</u> him true ...'

Isaiah 48:10: 'See, I have refined you though not as silver, I have <u>tested</u> you in the furnace of affliction.'

Daniel 11:35: 'Some of the wise will stumble, so that they may be <u>refined</u>, purified and made spotless until the time of the end ...'

Uses of *bachan* and *tsaraph* (and derivatives) together

Psalm 17:3: 'though you <u>probe</u> (*bachan*) my heart, though you examine me at night and <u>test</u> me (*tsaraph*) you will find that I have planned no evil'

Psalm 66:10: 'For you God <u>tested</u> (*bachan*) us, you <u>refined</u> (*tsaraph*) us like silver. You brought us into prison and laid burdens on our backs.'

Zechariah 13:9: 'I will refine (*tsaraph*) them like silver and <u>test</u> (*bachan*) them like gold. They will call on my Name and I will answer them. I will say "these are my people" and they will say "the LORD is our God"'

Note: all three words occur in Psalm 26:2: 'Test (*bachan*) me LORD, and try (*nasah*) me, examine (*tsaraph*) my heart and my mind, for I have always been mindful of your unfailing love ...'

NEW TESTAMENT ... Greek words

Dokimazo and derivatives

1 Corinthians 3:13: '... the fire will <u>test</u> the quality of each person's work ...'

2 Corinthians 8:8: 'I want to <u>test</u> the sincerity of your love ...'

1 Thessalonians 2:4: 'On the contrary we speak as those approved by God to be entrusted with the gospel. We are not trying to please people but God, who <u>tests</u> our hearts.'

Puroomi and derivatives

Revelation 3:18: 'I counsel you to buy me gold <u>refined</u> in the fire ...'

Peirasmos and derivatives

Matthew 4:1: 'Then Jesus was led by the Spirit into the wilderness to be <u>tempted</u> by the devil.' (see also Mark 1:13 and Luke 4:2)

Matthew 4:3: 'The <u>tempter</u> came to him and said ...'

Matthew 6:13 and Luke 11:4: '... lead us not into <u>temptation</u> ...'

Matthew 26:41; Mark 14:38; Luke 22:40, 46: 'Watch and pray so that you will not fall into <u>temptation</u>.'

'Luke 4:13: 'when the devil had finished all this <u>tempting</u> ...'

Luke 8:13: 'in the time of **testing** they fall away'

John 6:5, 6: ... (Jesus) 'said to Philip, "Where shall we buy bread for these people?" He asked this only to <u>test</u> him for he already had in mind what he was going to do ...'

1 Corinthians 7:5: 'Then come together again so that Satan will not <u>tempt</u> you because of your lack of self control.'

1 Corinthians 10:13: 'God is faithful he will not let you be <u>tempted</u> (NIV footnote 'tested') beyond what you can bear.'

Galatians 6:1: '... watch yourselves or you also may be <u>tempted</u>.'

1 Thessalonians 3:5: 'I was afraid that in some way the tempter had <u>tempted</u> you.'

1 Timothy 6:9: 'Those who want to get rich fall into <u>temptation</u> and a trap ...'

Hebrews 2:18: 'Because he himself suffered when he was tempted, he is able to help those who are being tempted ...'

Hebrews 3:8: '... do not harden your hearts as you did in the rebellion in the time of testing in the wilderness ...'

Hebrews 4:15: '(he) has been tempted in every way just as we are ...'

James 1:2: 'Consider it pure joy, my brothers and sisters, whenever you face trials (*peirasmois*) of many kinds because you know that the testing (*dokimon*) of your faith produces perseverance.'

James 1:12,13: 'Blessed is the one who perseveres under trial (*peirasmon*) because, having stood the test (*dokimos*), that person will receive the crown of life ...'

1 Peter 1:6: 'In all this you greatly rejoice, though now for a little while you may have had to suffer grief in all kinds of trials (*peirasmois*). These have come so that the proven (*dokimon*) genuineness of your faith—of greater worth than gold, which perishes even though refined (*dokimazonemou*) by fire—may result in praise, glory and honour when Jesus Christ is revealed.'

1 Peter 4:12: '... do not be surprised at the fiery ordeal (*purosei*) that has come on you to test (*peirasmon*) you as though something strange were happening to you ...'

2 Peter 2;9: '... the Lord knows how to rescue the godly from trials (*peirasmou*) ...'

Revelation 2:2: '... you have tested (*epeiorasas*) those who claim to be apostles but are not ...'

Revelation 2:10: 'the devil will put some of you in prison to test (*peirasthete*) you ...'

Revelation 3:10: 'Since you have kept my command to endure patiently, I will also keep you from the hour of trial that is going to come on the whole world to test the inhabitants of the earth.'

Also available from Christian Focus Publications...

HEALTH

WEALTH

AND THE

(REAL) GOSPEL

THE PROSPERITY GOSPEL MEETS THE TRUTHS OF SCRIPTURE

SEAN DeMARS AND MIKE McKINLEY

978-1-5271-0802-8

Health, Wealth, and the (Real) Gospel

The Prosperity Gospel Meets the Truths of Scripture

Sean DeMars and Mike McKinley

Having experienced its damaging effects, Sean DeMars and Mike McKinley set out to reveal the insidious toxicity found in the prosperity gospel. Naming and claiming promises of material blessing for those who believe enough may seem at first glance to be biblical, but turn out to be a distortion of God's truth.

Beginning by countering claims made by the prosperity gospel with what scripture actually teaches, they highlight the places in scripture that stand directly opposed to prosperity teachings. They explore what the Bible teaches about whether people who believe false doctrine are eternally saved, and how to examine our hearts for a prosperity-style understanding of God.

I am so grateful for this book by Sean DeMars and Michael Mckinley. It is a very readable and thoroughly biblical exposure of the complete theological bankruptcy of one of the most egregious distortions of the Gospel ever to disgrace the name of Christ.

Justin Peters, Founder of Justin Peters Ministries

Sean and Michael have written an honest and illuminating book that uses scripture (in context!) to confront all the core tenets of the prosperity gospel. It is also written in a way that is conversational, speaking the truth with directness in love. I pray the Lord will use this work to graciously reveal the glory of the true Christ to those in deception.

Brandon Kimber, Director of 'American Gospel: Christ Alone'

... insightful and humorous, wise and winsome, direct yet careful. I pray that God will cause your soul to prosper as you read this book.

Mark Dever, Senior Pastor, Capitol Hill Baptist Church and President, 9Marks.org, Washington, DC

Rich Grace
IN POOR SOIL

GROWING IN THE MASTER'S GRIP

Kenneth B. Wingate

978-1-5271-0806-6

Christian Focus Publications

Our mission statement –

STAYING FAITHFUL

In dependence upon God we seek to impact the world through literature faithful to His infallible Word, the Bible. Our aim is to ensure that the Lord Jesus Christ is presented as the only hope to obtain forgiveness of sin, live a useful life and look forward to heaven with Him.

Our books are published in four imprints:

CHRISTIAN
FOCUS

Popular works including biographies, commentaries, basic doctrine and Christian living.

CHRISTIAN
HERITAGE

Books representing some of the best material from the rich heritage of the church.

MENTOR

Books written at a level suitable for Bible College and seminary students, pastors, and other serious readers. The imprint includes commentaries, doctrinal studies, examination of current issues and church history.

CF4•K

Children's books for quality Bible teaching and for all age groups: Sunday school curriculum, puzzle and activity books; personal and family devotional titles, biographies and inspirational stories – because you are never too young to know Jesus!

Christian Focus Publications Ltd,
Geanies House, Fearn, Ross-shire,
IV20 1TW, Scotland, United Kingdom.
www.christianfocus.com

Rich Grace in Poor Soil

Growing in the Master's Grip

Kenneth B. Wingate

The garden provides the perfect image for the work of grace in our lives. In fact, Scripture often uses plant-based metaphors to describe the life of the believer. From the planting of the gospel seed to growing into oaks of righteousness, Kenneth Wingate explores these different aspects to show how we can flourish in Christ and bear fruit for Him.

One of the most frequently used metaphors in the Bible to picture the Christian life is that of the vineyard producing fruit. Kenneth Wingate has done an excellent job drawing upon this rich imagery to convey the clear teaching of Scripture concerning our growing in grace. Easy to understand, yet challenging to live, this book will be a great help to your pursuit of personal holiness. May God use it to bring forth much fruit in your life.

Steven J. Lawson, President, OnePassion Ministries and Professor of Preaching,The Master's Seminary, Sun Valley, California

Ken Wingate wants you to wallow in grace. In this manual for the Christian life he writes of deep grace with such a light touch—and good sense. Insights abound; the book is simply fun to read.

Dale Ralph Davis, Respected Author and Old Testament Scholar

Rich Grace in Poor Soil leads you to the very heart of God. For anyone who feels bruised, hurt or worn out, this book will refresh the soul. Written with a sharpness of insight and a flair for illustration, Rich Grace in Poor Soil is a tonic.

Derek W. H. Thomas, Senior Minister of Preaching and Teaching, First Presbyterian Church, Columbia, South Carolina

D0101429